Praises
Prayers &
Curses

Conversations with the
PSALMS

Richard H. Schmidt

Praises
Prayers &
Curses

Conversations with the
PSALMS

Forward Movement
Cincinnati, Ohio

Book design: Carole Miller
Jacket design: Robert W. Grove

FORWARD MOVEMENT
300 WEST FOURTH STREET
CINCINNATI, OHIO 45202-2666 USA

Forward Movement, an official, non-profit agency of The Episcopal
Church, is sustained through sales and tax-free contributions from
our readers.

Contents

Foreword

This book began with a few sheets of paper in a drawer. Some years ago, I began reading the Psalms straight through, from beginning to end, as part of my daily devotions. I was surprised at what I found. There was a lot of prayer and praise, as I had expected, but I also found perplexing, unsettling, even vicious things. When I came across something like that, I often reached for a pen and paper and jotted down a few thoughts. The result was a small stack of papers containing random reflections on verses in the Psalms. My imagination took free rein in these jottings, wandering where it would. Sometimes I recalled an incident from an earlier time in my life which the psalm brought to mind. Some thoughts related to events in the news of the day. Some pertained to theological or ethical dilemmas. Occasionally I included a quotation which the psalm suggested to me or imagined a dialogue in my mind with the psalmist or with God. These reflections became the nucleus for an issue of the devotional magazine *Forward Day by Day* (December 2001 and January 2002). The editor later invited me to expand them into a collection of meditations on each of the 150 psalms. This is the result.

Many people's exposure to the Psalms is limited to Sunday worship. This is unfortunate. For one thing, too many parishes rush through the psalm on Sunday morning, as if the main thing is to finish so as to move on to something else. Read that way, the words have no time to sink in. Moreover, the compilers of the three-year Sunday lectionary which the Episcopal Church shares with other Christians attacked the Psalter with their scissors. As a result, most worshipers today get mere snippets of psalms, and most of what they get is lofty, edifying, comforting—and above all, inoffensive. That's all very well, but what about the plaintive cries, the railings at God, the racism, and the vindictive curses? The liturgical gurus, apparently thinking those passages unsuitable for Sunday worship, snipped them out.

I have come to appreciate those perplexing, strange, and violent passages. Sometimes I disagree with the psalmists and want to shake my finger at them, but I like their honesty, the fact that they sugar-coat nothing. The Psalter contains every possible human emotion, from the lofty to the base, from the noble to the disgusting. That means that whatever I am feeling, I can always find a psalmist who understands. The psalmists have become my companions, both in sadness and in joy, in anger and in gratitude. Whatever happens to me, I can always say, "I am not the first to have walked this way. The psalmist has already been here."

This book is not a commentary on the Psalms, nor does it much rely on the commentaries of others. I consulted a commentary only when I found myself stuck about the meaning of a word or some other technical point. That's not because I have no use for commentaries—far from it. Anyone undertaking a serious study of the Psalter must consider questions of authorship, the meaning of Hebrew words, the structure of Hebrew poetry, psalm types, the setting in which the psalms were originally sung, and the place of these songs in the Bible and in Jewish and Christian worship. Dozens of good commentaries offer this information, but this book isn't one of them.

I hope the meditations in this book will be useful to others who enjoy reflecting on the Psalms. You may find them a spur to your own reflections. That is, after all, how these meditations came to be written. I suggest daily reading of the Psalter, at a quiet, leisurely time set aside for that purpose. I use the scheme found in the Book of Common Prayer

(I also use the Prayer Book translation, which accounts for the occasional differences from other translations in verse numbers since the Prayer Book versification is designed to facilitate singing). Using this scheme, the entire Psalter is completed in 30 days for those who read twice a day, or 60 days for those who read once a day. That gives about 40 to 50 verses for each reading, which is plenty. Half that would be quite enough. So as not to be rushed (meaningful meditation is not possible when rushed), allow at least 15 minutes, preferably longer, when you read the Psalms. Let your soul dance around the words and phrases and do not restrain your mind from wandering where it will. Sometimes the most unlikely connections prove the most fruitful for meditation.

The Psalter was not compiled for individual meditation, however, but for group use. It is a collection of 150 hymns and poems for singing in corporate worship. It is often called "the hymnbook of the temple." That's because the collection, after centuries of editing and revising, came into its present form during the time of the Second Temple, the temple of Zerubbabel, in the late 6th century B.C. These songs were sung in worship there—and they are still sung in corporate worship. The Psalter is therefore a communal book, much like a modern hymnal. Although some of the Psalms seem to have been written by individuals about particular events in their lives, they are in the Bible because they expressed the mind of a worshiping community.

Small groups may also enjoy meditating on the Psalms. In the parish where I served as rector until 2000, we began every vestry meeting with a group reflection on a psalm. I distributed copies of a psalm or part of a psalm. We then read the psalm slowly, pausing a beat after each half verse—I cannot overemphasize again, the importance of reading at an unhurried pace. Then we took three minutes for everyone in the group to consider two questions: What can I guess or surmise about the psalmist and the psalmist's circumstances? Where do my life and my experiences intersect with the psalmist's? Each person then selected a verse, phrase, or image from the psalm that was especially suggestive to him or her. Then we shared our selections with the group and briefly discussed them. A few of the meditations in this book arose out of those discussions.

Finally, I am grateful to my wife Pamela and to my friend Howard Park for reading the initial draft of these meditations and making helpful suggestions to improve content and clarity.

Richard H. Schmidt
Chesterfield, Missouri
January, 2005

Book One

☙

Psalms 1 through 41

*Happy are they who have not walked in the
counsel of the wicked,
nor lingered in the way of sinners,
nor sat in the seats of the scornful!
Their delight is in the law of the LORD,
and they meditate on his law day and night.*

The Book of Psalms opens with a discussion of happiness, a topic addressed often in the Psalter and from a variety of perspectives. Human beings everywhere pursue happiness, but where is happiness found? The psalmist discusses the answer in terms of two "lifestyles," using a vivid image to describe each.

First are those who delight in the ways of the Lord and meditate day and night upon them. These, says the psalmist, flourish like trees planted in the rich river bottomland. They bear fruit and their leaves do not wither. The wicked, on the other hand, are like chaff blown away in the wind. It is possible to interpret these two images literally (as some biblical authors, including some of the psalmists, do), as if good people are guaranteed a happy life while bad people will be knocked off their feet. Other biblical authors (including many of the psalmists we shall meet) and thoughtful people generally are quick to point out that experience does not support this view.

Perhaps the psalm is intended to lead the reader to ask what really brings happiness. Many, then as now, seek happiness in more and bigger things—houses, cars, stock portfolios, careers, reputations. Some who succeed in this effort find that their abundance leaves them feeling as empty and lost as before. This opening psalm suggests we seek happiness in thinking as God thinks, day and night, all the time, in letting the mind of God saturate our souls. Those who do this are like trees planted by streams of water, flourishing in every way that matters. Those who turn their minds to other things amount to nothing in the end.

℘ 2.1a

Why are the nations in an uproar?

That's a good question. Here are three possible answers:

The nations are in an uproar because we (it is not just other nations, of course) mistake what is merely pleasing for what is good, and what is merely good for what is supremely good. We don't know the true worth of things. Our values are upside-down, out of kilter, blurred.

The nations are in an uproar because these upside-down values of ours lead us into regions not worth traveling to. We wander through what Bunyan named Vanity Fair and Eliot called "this stony rubbish," where trinkets are passed off for treasures and brackish water for fresh. The travel brochures offered pretty pictures and we believed them—but the promise proved an empty one. We seek what our souls long for, but we don't know what our souls need, so we seek in all the wrong places. We are lost, often without knowing it, and we can't find our way back.

The nations are in an uproar because we not only wander in the wrong places, but wear blinders that block out much of what is good and beautiful even in those places. Goodness and beauty can be found even in prison cells and hospital rooms where death waits in the wings—I know because I have found them there. But if we concentrate only on the vacant faces of those who are as lost as we are and listen only to the petty patter of their aimless chatter, we may mistakenly assume that's all there is—and we're bright enough to realize that's not much.

And so, along with the rest of the nations, we are in an uproar. We clamor and claw for our rights, our dignity, our due. We complain that we've been cheated. And so we have been. But by whom?

෬ 3.5

I lie down and go to sleep;
I wake again, because the LORD sustains me.

This psalm and the next four introduce a theme which we shall meet again and again in the Psalter—the psalmist's enemies and his prayers about them. These psalms display a number of common features, but the tone and emphasis vary from one to another. As in most cases, this psalmist tells us something about his enemies but does not identify them. "They" mock his trust in God; and there are many of them—but who are *they?* The lack of identification of enemies invites us to personalize these psalms by supplying these adversaries with faces and names drawn from our own lives, thereby making the psalmists' prayers our own. Our most vicious adversaries often lie within us, in the form of brooding resentments, imaginary slights, and empty vanities that corrode our souls.

In this psalm we see the paradoxical range of feelings people experience when they feel attacked. The psalmist wants to lash out—or better, have God lash out on his behalf—at those who afflict him. But on the other hand, the psalmist speaks of his quiet confidence in the Lord which enables him to enjoy a restful sleep. These two very different thoughts, vengefulness and quiet confidence, often alternate, with first one and then the other taking center stage, in the mind of someone confronting "many adversaries."

The psalmist apparently does, at least some of the time, sleep soundly; he does not experience restless nights. The reason, he says, is that the Lord sustains him. Of course, the Lord sustains him—the Lord sustains everyone, including the psalmist, his adversaries, you and me, everyone. But when fear of enemies begins to gnaw at us, we cannot be still because in our minds we hear no voices but those of our adversaries. It's one thing for the Lord to sustain us, but we sleep restfully only when we *acknowledge* that the Lord sustains us.

Many are saying,
"Oh, that we might see better times!"

"As soon as I get a better job...as soon as I find a wife who understands me...as soon as I can move somewhere else...as soon as I get more money, more friends, more self-confidence, more education, more faith!" Scorning the present moment, we grow discontented, angry, and resentful. We assign God a timetable to do things for us. "God, listen to me! I need you to fix this right now!" We hear no response because we don't want to hear the response: "*You* listen to *me*. What I have in mind for you doesn't include my fixing that problem, not now, maybe not ever. Why don't you learn to wait? Why don't you learn to enjoy the present moment?"

The present moment usually contains many blessings, but if we think only of what is unpleasant in the present or about what we want done in the future, we can't enjoy anything. God is already with us in the present moment, pleasant or unpleasant, and if we would find him, it will be there. The present moment contains all that there is. Any blessing we receive will be received only in its time, when its moment becomes the present moment.

The eighteenth century spiritual director Jean Pierre de Caussade said it well in his book, *Abandonment to Divine Providence*: "We can find all that is necessary in the present moment. We need not worry about whether to pray or be silent, whether to withdraw into retreat or mix with people, to read or write, to meditate or make our minds a receptive blank, to shun or seek out books on spirituality. Nor do poverty or riches, sickness or health, life or death matter in the least. What does matter is what each moment produces by the will of God."

❦ 4.8

I lie down in peace; at once I fall asleep...

I usually fall quickly to sleep at night. A good night's sleep can't be taken for granted, and I thank God for it. When I can't sleep, however, it is often because something is out of balance in my soul. I ask myself these questions when sleep eludes me:

Am I angry at someone? Nothing interferes with sleep as quickly as anger. It doesn't merely *exist* in the soul—it *burns* in the soul, making it impossible to "lie down in peace." Sometimes I fall to sleep quickly but then awaken at 3:00 a.m. with my stomach in knots. It's anger that does that to me. I get up and pray for the person at whom I am angry and ask God to banish the anger from my soul. I visualize God's healing warmth and forgiveness surrounding that person. I often must do this over and over since anger does not readily accept banishment.

Am I impatient? I often chafe at the time it takes to get things done working with volunteers, who can be unreliable and understand a task differently than I do. Then I remind myself that a thousand years in God's sight are like an evening and that even if something isn't done when or the way I want, the sun will still rise tomorrow—I guess I can wait.

Do I take myself too seriously? Most things are less important than I think they are, including my own opinions and desires, and a century from now, God will still be God and the things that keep me awake at night won't matter to me or to anyone else. They will, in fact, have been entirely and mercifully forgotten.

Am I obedient? When I refuse to look at something in my life which God is calling me to examine, I grow tense and withdrawn, and I can't sleep. Becoming honest with God and myself and asking God to purify my will restores harmony to my soul and enables me to lie down in peace.

ೞ 5.3

In the morning, LORD, you hear my voice;
early in the morning I make my appeal and
watch for you.

Like the psalmist, as I have grown older, I have gravitated to early morning as my prayer time, and like the psalmist, I too pray for justice in a world where evil seems so often to have the upper hand and the innocent suffer long and needlessly. I am not as confident as this psalmist, however, that the wicked and the righteous can be sorted out into two groups. The innocent and the guilty are the same persons, and culpability is a matter of degree—*all* have sinned and fallen short of the glory of God, as St. Paul says. Those who cheat and steal are more obviously wicked than their victims, but no human soul is pure and undefiled.

After a few moments of quiet recollection, I begin my morning prayer time by confessing my own sins (to the extent that I know them) and asking to be washed, healed, repaired, and made new in the likeness of Christ. I try not to dwell on the sins of others, even when they impinge on me personally. Then I offer up to God situations known to me where justice seems denied and the innocent are victimized. Whether God deals with the offenders by declaring them guilty and punishing them, as this and other psalmists call for, I leave to God to decide. Perhaps God will choose instead to bring the wicked to repentance and newness of life.

When I have completed my early morning prayers and intercessions, I am ready for breakfast and the morning newspaper. Usually there is little in the paper to give thanks for, perhaps because there is so much goodness in the world that goodness is not newsworthy. I find that having prayed before reading the day's news makes it easier to read about all the things that have gone wrong in the world during the past 24 hours.

❧ 6.2-3

Have pity on me, LORD, for I am weak;
heal me, LORD, for my bones are racked.
My spirit shakes with terror;
how long, O LORD, how long?

This is one of seven psalms which the ancient church called the "penitential psalms." The others are psalms 32, 38, 51,

102, 130, and 143. These psalms are woeful and plaintive. On rare occasions, I have prayed one of the penitential psalms because I shared the feelings expressed in them. With dark clouds extending over my mental horizon in every direction, I have moaned, "How long, O Lord, how long?" I tend to withdraw into isolation from other people, even those who would help me, when pain, physical or emotional, becomes intense for me. I endure my misery alone. Is that what this psalmist was doing? We don't have to withhold our sympathy or minimize the psalmist's pain to recognize a certain self-preoccupation here, nor are we required to regard every thought expressed in the psalm as a healthy or laudable one.

Although it ends on a note of hope, this psalm is mostly a cry of despair. We are not told the psalmist's actual circumstances—references to pain in his bones and to "my enemies" may be metaphorical. We don't know the cause of the psalmist's grief, but we get the feel of it: He is afraid that God will rebuke and punish him. He does not believe in life after death. He is weary from groaning and has drenched his bed with his tears. He sees no end to his misery.

Perhaps a hint of the way out of the psalmist's malaise is found in verse 9 where he acknowledges that "the Lord accepts my prayer." His prayer may be shriveled and self-pitying, but the Lord accepts it. The Lord accepts all prayers, even when the faith behind them is battered and drained. The assurance that the Lord accepts even an unworthy and inadequate prayer has carried me through several desperate moments.

Stand up, O LORD, in your wrath;
    rise up against the fury of my enemies.

Several ideas are woven together in this psalm: The psalmist's enemies seek his violent destruction. The Lord always saves the innocent. The psalmist is completely innocent and therefore calls upon the Lord to defend and deliver him. He is confident that the Lord will see that the evil of the psalmist's enemies will come back upon them.

Taken together, I find these ideas unsettling. As so often, we know nothing of the specific circumstances which gave rise to this psalm, but if I could engage the psalmist in a conversation, I'd like to say a few things to him and ask him a few questions:

You seem absolutely certain that you have done nothing wrong. There are instances where one party is clearly innocent and another clearly guilty. Genocide comes to mind. Political torture. Government corruption. Abusive behavior of all kinds. But few things are as simple as they seem, and there are two sides to most stories. *Is there another side to your story? How would your enemies tell the tale?*

God moves in many and mysterious ways, often hidden from us. He seems to have a longer tolerance for evil than many of us have. Sometimes God uses evil to bring good from it. Sometimes God allows evil to continue for reasons known only to him. Sometimes he seems to be silent or absent when we most want to see and hear him. You could ask fellow biblical author Job about that. *Could there be things about the ways of God that you do not discern?*

There are various ways to deal with malicious opposition. One possibility is to obliterate it, or if that is not within your power, to call upon God to obliterate it. Another is to resist passively. Another is to suffer quietly and pray. Another is to work to undermine the opposition or to convert the opposition. You could even forgive your enemies. *Have you considered all your options?*

౼ 8.4-5

When I consider the heavens, the work of
your fingers,
the moon and the stars you have set in
their courses,
What is man that you should be mindful of him?
the son of man that you should seek him out?

Modern people know something of the measureless expanse of the universe which the author of this psalm could not have imagined. We know the earth to be a small planet circling a small star, one of billions of stars in a galaxy among billions of galaxies.

The suggestion that the Creator of the universe would seek out the inhabitants of this insignificant dot of a place is implausible; to suggest that the Creator would *become* one of us would seem a pretension beyond words. Such a suggestion would never have occurred to the psalmist, even with his limited knowledge of the cosmos—but it is precisely what

Christians say God has done, modern cosmology and astronomy notwithstanding.

Is the Christian claim absurd? Well, yes, it is absurd. To Muslims, the suggestion that God would stoop to such depths is blasphemous, insulting the very name of God. Let us not pretend that our faith is the sort of thing a reasonable person would come up with. There are only three possibilities: Christians are arrogant. Or they are stupid. Or the truth is stranger than reason. Far from being arrogant or stupid, the Christians who best exemplify their faith are notable for their humility and wisdom. That would seem to recommend the third possibility.

☙ 9.1

I will give thanks to you, O Lord, with my whole heart;
I will tell of all your marvelous works.

Most of us, if we give thanks at all, do not give thanks with our *whole* heart, for *all* God's marvelous works. Rather, we are thankful only for the pleasant things in our lives. But consider that God's "marvelous works" may include even unhappy, difficult things. Try giving thanks for the following:

Failure. Most people don't like to fail. It would be strange if they did. But failure can teach us that what we think is the end is never really the end. Resurrection is always possible, but you must be crucified first.

Poverty. Some people devote their lives to getting more, bigger, and better of everything, then wonder why their lives seem empty and meaningless. Meaning comes when we are filled with God, which is possible only when we have emptied ourselves of what doesn't matter, so as to receive him.

Infirmity. It is easier for the weak to learn their dependence upon God than for the strong. I learned my dependence upon God only when I confessed my helplessness in the face of a terrifying and nearly fatal addiction. Now I give thanks for that addiction because of what it taught me.

Doubt. Doubt dogs me constantly. I have prayed God to remove doubt from my mind, but he does not do so. I am therefore learning to thank him for it. When the treasure is hidden out of sight, it is all the lovelier, and there is fresh energy for the search.

❧ 10.1

Why do you stand so far off, O Lord,
and hide yourself in time of trouble?

I have experienced little real trouble. Persecution, betrayal, starvation, chronic illness or disability—most of my troubles have been of a lesser sort. My grimmest trouble occurred some years ago when I had a job which paid well, but in which I felt cheapened and used. I became angry and withdrawn and nearly lost my faith. People who knew me questioned my mental stability. Inside, I felt parched and shriveled. I cried out to God but heard no response. Looking up at what I suspected was an empty heaven, I asked the question with which this psalm begins.

Only now, years later, have I gained a sense of why God stood so far off in my time of trouble—he didn't. God only seemed to stand far off because my fear and anger kept me from hearing his voice and seeing his face. Though I felt abandoned, in truth God was with me all along.

Could God have taken away my pain immediately, the moment I first cried out to him? Probably, but I might have chalked it up to good fortune and never known it was God who had come to me. I might not have acknowledged my helplessness before God and my need of his grace. God used my "trouble" to bring me to my senses. I now count that as a good time, because it drove me into the arms of God. But I'd still like to ask God, "Can't you find an easier way to teach me my lessons?"

↷ 11.3

*When the foundations are being destroyed,
what can the righteous do?*

Many loyal church people today feel the foundations are being destroyed: The Bible is little read and known. Christian values are increasingly ignored by secular society. Ideas once thought untrue and behaviors once thought immoral are widely accepted, even in the pews and the pulpit.

What can the righteous do? That is a dangerous question. Do we think of ourselves as the righteous? Are those who differ from us the unrighteous? And what are the foundations? Do our opinions on disputed points comprise the foundations on which the Kingdom of God must stand?

If we answer these questions in the affirmative, we sound like the Pharisees of old. They knew who and what was right, and they saw it when they gazed at themselves in the mirror. Modern Pharisees can be either liberals or conservatives. Pharisaical religion takes itself very seriously. It invites its adherents to idolize it, eliminating God and erecting a statue of itself in God's place. When our religion becomes an idol, then knowing, worshiping, and serving God takes a back seat to convincing everyone that our religion is the true one.

What can the righteous do? Pray. Trust God. Follow Christ, as Christ enables them to do. What are the foundations? The church's one foundation is Jesus Christ her Lord—and nothing anyone believes, says, or does can destroy him.

℘ 12.1a

...the faithful have vanished from among us.

People during my youth seemed more faithful than people today. Everyone in the small Southern town where I grew up agreed about questions of faith and morality, or so it seemed to me as a child. If there was disagreement or bickering in the church, I was unaware of it. All the persons in the pews were,

I assumed, faithful and godly souls who loved their Lord and each other. Now, years later, I ask myself:

Were things years ago really that different from today? I recall as a teenager hearing my grandmother criticize my generation, and I swore that when I grew older, I'd never speak negatively about the generation following mine. But now I understand how my grandmother felt, because the faithful seem to have vanished from among us—but does the older generation always think the younger one is faithless? Maybe the problem is that none of us think God can work except through people who do and think as we do.

Why not give thanks for the faithful people in our past—or at least for the fact that we remember them as faithful—rather than bemoan the scarcity of faithful people today? Focusing on the bad, the unpleasant, the misguided is sometimes necessary, but it can also breed negativity. How blessed I am that my memory is full of the faces and voices of faithful people!

What is faithfulness, anyway? If I assume that the faithful are people like me, I set myself up as the judge of faithfulness. But I could be wrong. Christ is the measure of faithfulness, and by that standard, every generation falls short. Some may even look at me and my generation and say, "the faithful have vanished from among us."

℘ 13.2

How long shall I have perplexity in my mind,
and grief in my heart, day after day?
how long shall my enemy triumph over me?

As a youngster, everything seemed clear to me. There were no ambiguities, no perplexing questions. I felt secure, comfortable, cozy with God because I knew who God was and what God wanted—and I felt confident that I was not far off the mark. But as an adult, I encountered baffling doubts and uncertainties, not only about my own worthiness, but about the will of God and the very reality of God. I longed for the return of the simple faith of childhood. How long would this perplexity continue?

The perplexity was partly intellectual—how could a good and powerful God create a world with so much suffering? If there is a God and he wishes to be known, why doesn't he communicate himself more clearly? What does it mean, exactly, to say that Jesus is divine, and how, exactly, does his death 2,000 years ago benefit me? But I came eventually to realize that my perplexity mainly arose not from asking difficult questions, which is neither uncommon nor unhealthy. Something deeper than questions was troubling my soul. My questioning may even have been a self-justifying device to deflect me from having to look at what I didn't want to see.

My enemy was not my questioning mind, but my rebellious will. I could know well enough the sort of relationship God desired with me—if I wanted to know. A simple look at Jesus would disclose it, intellectual doubts notwithstanding. But I didn't want to know—because I didn't want to change or allow God to change me. Only when we are willing to change and invite God to do his good pleasure in us, will the perplexity of our minds and the ache in our hearts abate.

℞ 14.3

Every one has proved faithless;
all alike have turned bad;
    there is none who does good; no, not one.

The first three verses of this psalm could have come from Diogenes, the dour Greek who groped patiently through Athens with his lantern in search of one solitary, honest soul. None was to be found. A pessimistic, cynical view of humanity oozes from these verses. They remind me of a horrible story I once heard, of a father who stood at the foot of the stairs, arms wide open, as his son ran down the stairs to leap into his arms. But the father stepped back at the last moment so that his son crashed to the floor. The father then said, "Didn't I warn you, son, never to trust *anybody*?" Someone who feels that way about other people will grab everything he can, and never mind anyone else. After all, if everyone is wicked, why not play the game the best you can?

I know a few people who really do feel that way. Some of them have managed to acquire a lot of money by dubious means. But I'm glad I don't see people as uniformly corrupt, even if it means I get hurt occasionally. My wife says I'm naive and sometimes asks, "Why do you always assume everyone will behave honorably? Why don't you protect yourself by playing your cards closer to your chest?" The reason, I suppose, is that when I look at someone, I'd rather see a hint of the goodness of God, even if it turns out I'm mistaken, than lack for a single real friend because I assume the worst of everyone I meet.

The concluding verses of the psalm seem to indicate that the psalmist doesn't actually believe that *everyone* is faithless and bad, because he refers to "the righteous" and "the afflicted," presumably the victims of the those mentioned earlier. He asks that God deliver and restore the righteous and the afflicted. I join the psalmist in that prayer—and let it be a prayer of deeds as well as a prayer of words.

꩜ 15.1-2

LORD, who may dwell in your tabernacle?
who may abide upon your holy hill?
Whoever leads a blameless life and does what
is right...

So are only the morally pure acceptable in the worshiping community? This psalm describes such a person as one who has no guile, does not heap contempt on others, honors the godly, keeps his word, is always honest. A noble soul, to be sure—but where is this person? I am yet to meet him. Most of us manifest such qualities some of the time, some of us even most of the time, but no one "leads a blameless life." Totally without blame? For anything? Ever? I think not.

If all are unworthy and only the worthy are acceptable,

then why do we not turn everyone away at the church door? The reason is that Jesus turned no one away. Jesus himself actually did manifest the qualities called for in this psalm, and yet opened his arms to sinners.

I am thinking of one of my parishioners and friends. He comes pretty close to manifesting the Christlike qualities described in this psalm. He shows compassion to the weak, the misunderstood, and the overlooked. When insulted, he quietly carries on. Often rejected, he accepts others as Christ accepted others, even those who avoid him. My friend is gay. I don't know the mind of God regarding homosexuality— godly people disagree about it and thoughtful arguments can be advanced for various positions. But I know that my friend discloses Christ to me. I see Jesus when I look into his face. Through my friend, God is leading me to a new understanding of virtuous living and of forgiveness and to recognize them in places I would once not have looked for them.

০ৎ 16.6

My boundaries enclose a pleasant land;
indeed, I have a goodly heritage.

How often we look longingly at another's land or heritage! Our insecurity demands that we compare what our boundaries enclose to what the boundaries of others enclose. Our income, house, car, wardrobe, spouse, job, reputation, circle of friends, or social position must equal or surpass that of the next person. If it does not, we tell ourselves we have not received our due. We feel like failures and we grow angry and resentful.

Congregations do the same thing. Two congregations in the same neighborhood often behave as competitors. If one wins, the other must lose. They compare size, friendliness, programs, theology. Neither seems willing simply to be the people God calls them to be and allow the other congregation to be the people God calls them to be. Each wants to be bigger or better or more faithful than its neighbor. Clergy sometimes get caught up in this game of comparison. One of the most liberating moments of my life occurred when I declined a call to become rector of a large and wealthy parish and chose instead to go to a small, out-of-the-way, low-paying parish because it seemed the more honest and faithful of the two. I had made a conscious decision to stop playing the game of comparison.

The game of comparison has no winners. There will always be someone with more of what we want. The secret to a contented life is to look to what God has given us and find within it the beauty and goodness of its Maker. St. Paul learned, even while in a prison cell, to be content with what he had (Phil. 4:11). Julian of Norwich, the 13th century mystic, saw infinite beauties in a hazel nut, and Thomas Traherne, the 17th century poet, saw the same in a grain of sand and a kernel of corn.

∝ 17.3

Weigh my heart, summon me by night,
melt me down; you will find no impurity
in me.

The psalmist faces enemies who act like lions seeking their prey. He protests his innocence, and at some length. When people do that, I sometimes wonder why they talk on and on about how blameless they are—a hint of humility would be welcome. And yet, for all the self-justification it contains, this psalm also rings with an authentic sense of dependence and intimacy with God.

Perhaps the key to that paradox is found in the source of the psalmist's purity. He never says it's due to his own righteousness. He envisions himself as a piece of pottery, a common biblical metaphor. I am reminded of the spiritual song: "Spirit of the living God, fall afresh on me. Break me, melt me, mold me, fill me. Spirit of the living God, fall afresh on me." Someone, apparently disliking the thought of getting broken, changed the middle line to "Melt me, mold me, fill me, use me." The revised wording contains nothing objectionable, but I prefer the original because in my case (and I suspect in every case), something needed breaking. Call it ego, will, the old self, whatever—but until it is broken (that really is the best word), we are spiritually stuck, spinning our wheels in a muddy hole, going nowhere.

After the pot is broken and only then, it can be melted down, its impurities refined away. It is then remolded into a new shape—and filled. It becomes a new creation. That's what God does for us, in us, with us, when we surrender to him and invite him to have his way with us. Then we can join the psalmist in saying, "you will find no impurity in me."

✑ 18.4,6,8

The breakers of death rolled over me,
  and the torrents of oblivion made me
    afraid....
I called upon the LORD in my distress
  and cried out to my God for help....
The earth reeled and rocked;
  the roots of the mountains shook;
  they reeled because of his anger.

I lay awake for hours in the equatorial heat. As a boy growing up in the American South, I had known how to deal with such heat—walk slowly, drink lots of water, and shower several times a day. But then air conditioning transformed the South, and I forgot how to survive the heat. Now, as a middle-aged man accustomed to artificially controlled temperatures, I found myself in a distant land with no fan, no air conditioner, no breeze—just the sultry heat, humidity, and mosquitoes. A pool of perspiration collected in the center of my bed and my limbs stuck to my sides. As dawn approached and still I could not sleep, I decided to get up and read the Psalms, as I do at home when sleep eludes me. I turned to this psalm.

"The breakers of death rolled over me, and the torrents of oblivion made me afraid." Well, that puts things in perspective, doesn't it? This psalmist had to deal with the breakers of death and the torrents of oblivion—and I complain because *it's too hot for me to sleep?* "The earth reeled and rocked, the roots of the mountains shook; they reeled because of his anger." That's what the Lord did for the psalmist when he cried out; is my discomfort such that I'd want a remedy *like that?* Well, I suppose not. If I think it's hard to go to sleep now, wouldn't all that reeling and rocking and shaking just make matters worse? No, thank you, Lord, I don't care for that kind of relief. I guess I'll just go back to bed. I'll sleep if I can and quit my bellyaching if I can't. If a sleepless night now and then is all I have to grouse about, I've got a lot of nerve complaining at all.

℘ 18.29

You, O LORD, are my lamp;
my God, you make my darkness bright.

Once, many years ago, I had occasion to spend the night with a friend who lived in the basement of an old rooming house. It was nearly 10 p.m. when I arrived, and no one was there. The entryway was dark. I entered and felt on the wall for a light switch. I found none. Hesitantly, I stepped into the darkness, moving my hands in the air before me to avoid bumping into something. I felt my way along a wall, eventually finding what I guessed was the door to my friend's room. I entered. Still I could see nothing. I began to feel vaguely frightened. I bumped into a chair, then a desk—surely there would be a light on the desk. Yes! My hand touched a lamp. I turned the switch, and the light came on.

Looking around me, I saw that the room contained a couch and a desk, an easy chair and a bed, familiar, ordinary objects, hardly things to be afraid of. I felt silly at having been frightened. The light had transformed a murky, ominous place into an orderly, benign place.

Christ is the floodlight who illumines all things. Dangers are not removed, but become part of a larger picture, full of grace and truth. This includes the dangers that lurk within us—bitterness, resentment, self-will. When exposed to the light of Christ, their grip is broken and they terrorize us no more.

ॐ 19.5

In the deep he has set a pavilion for the sun;
it comes forth like a bridegroom out of his
chamber;
it rejoices like a champion to run its course.

Most modern Western people have lost a sense of the winsomeness of natural phenomena. We may comment on the beauty of a sunset or a mountain vista, but we relate to nature primarily as matter, as stuff. Even when we acknowledge beauty in nature, we see it as something to dig up, cut down, bottle, photograph or shrink wrap, and then take home with us. Sometimes we hang it on our wall.

This verse gives us a charming and quite different picture. Whereas we today think of the sun as a mass of hydrogen and helium 93 million miles distant, the psalmist imagines the sun as a bridegroom full of youthful vigor, radiating a brassy self-confidence as he bursts from his wedding chamber, or as the victor of an athletic contest strutting to the winner's circle. A few verses earlier, the psalmist envisions each day telling a story to the next, each night passing on to its successor the wisdom it has learned.

Such images are not to be taken literally, of course, and the psalmist knew that. But I expect he took quite seriously the notion that natural phenomena are *alive*. Just as God created human beings in his own image, imparting to us something of his divine nature, so too he created the rest of the natural order and implanted something of himself in it. Like human beings, nature resonates with the life, imagination, and the winsomeness of its Creator.

℘ 19.12

Who can tell how often he offends?
cleanse me from my secret faults.

The devil does not have horns and a tail, wear red leotards, or carry a pitchfork. That would make him easy to recognize. His method is to disguise himself as the agent of virtue. His (her?) counsel seems reasonable and fair; his singing sounds like hymnody. The result is that the very things about ourselves which we feel are most commendable are often our most grievous sins, eating away our souls' health and keeping us outside the arms of God.

The Seven Deadly Sins of medieval moral theology can all be dressed up as virtues: Pride is called self-fulfillment. Anger is justified on grounds of our having been denied our due. Envy and avarice form the foundation of an entire economic system. Sloth is called a disease and the slothful its victims. Gluttony and lust are promoted on the airwaves, in theaters, and in glossy magazines. Yielding to sin becomes normal behavior, accepted everywhere and rarely questioned, even in churches. A nation's soul withers and decays.

If we were handed a certified list of our offenses, we could at least consider repentance. But so long as we perceive our sins as virtues, there is nothing of which to repent. Repentance includes the willingness to change. The first step is to repent of our known sins and ask for the grace to amend our ways, but then we must move deeper and ask to be cleansed from those insidious spiritual poisons of which we are not even aware.

൙ 20.4

May the LORD...grant you your heart's desire, and prosper all your plans.

The concluding verses of this psalm make clear that these words are spoken to the king and refer to his military campaigns. It is well that we pray for our leaders and their plans, but this verse, and the three that precede it, can be spoken of anyone undertaking a risky endeavor. Some risks are too great for the reward sought and others are foolhardy and shouldn't be taken for any reason. But most people, at least once in their lives, are given an opportunity to take a risk in order to pursue a dream, and the risk is often worth taking.

I took such a risk once, undertaking a work I had long dreamt of doing, but which required that I take a 40 percent cut in pay. It was difficult, but it was the right decision and I am glad I did it. At the time I write these words, two of my sons, now grown, have decided to take similar risks. One is turning his back on a tenured position with little chance of advancement to move to a city with more employment opportunities but where he does not now have a job. The other is taking a low paying position with a company he has long wanted to work for, hoping for a promotion with higher pay in due time. Although these decisions will take my sons from within five minutes of where my wife and I live to cities hundreds of miles distant, I applaud their vision and courage and give them my blessing. I would speak the words of this psalm to them.

There are some questions to ask, though: Just what is "your heart's desire?" What are "all your plans?" Some desires and some plans ought not to be pursued. Is your heart's desire merely to have a good time or to gain power or fame or money for yourself? Or will it enable you to serve and enjoy God more fully? Are your plans consistent with God's plans?

℘ 21.2

You have given him his heart's desire;
you have not denied him the request of
his lips.

This psalm reads like a sequel to the one before it, after the request made in that psalm has been granted. It appears that the military victory sought in Psalm 20 has now been won. Few modern readers of these two psalms will be reigning monarchs or military commanders, but the words of both psalms can also be appropriated by persons of lesser rank.

How do you respond when you experience what is usually called "good fortune?" You recover from an illness. You receive a coveted appointment or award. The woman you love agrees to marry you. A healthy child is born. Good fortune makes us happy, and we often celebrate in some way. But do we pause to thank God for it?

The phrase "good fortune" carries a connotation of chance, of coincidence, and I do not deny that chance and coincidence are part of life as God has set up the world. But that is not the whole truth. In some way beyond our understanding, operating alongside good fortune, is the power of God, working in history and the lives of people to bring good things to pass. This is usually called grace or providence. I have never known how to sort out the relationship between good fortune and divine providence, so I simply let the discontinuity stand as a paradox. But like the king in this psalm, when good things happen in my life, I know where they come from, and I rejoice not merely in good fortune, but in the power of the Lord who gives me my heart's desire.

ᘓ 22.1

My God, my God, why have you forsaken me?
and are so far from my cry
and from the words of my distress?

Christians will immediately recognize here Jesus' cry of abandonment from the cross. It is likely that Jesus, who knew the Psalms well, had in mind all of Psalm 22 when he spoke its opening words from the cross. Many details of the psalm suggest the specific circumstances of Jesus' death, and the opening words would have brought the entire psalm to his mind, much as the words "Our Father" bring the complete text of the Lord's Prayer to the mind of a modern Christian who knows the prayer by heart.

When contemplating a saying or incident in Jesus' life, I often ask whether it speaks more intently to me if I think of it in connection with Jesus' divine nature or in connection with his human nature. In the case of his uttering this psalm from the cross, I think of it both ways.

Jesus was a human being. Most of us feel forsaken by God from time to time. We feel either that God is real but has turned his back on us, or that the God we had thought was real is actually an illusion. The feeling of abandonment is the same. Jesus, being fully human, also felt abandoned by the God in whom he had trusted. When we feel that way, we are not alone—Jesus, one of us, has visited that forsaken place and is present with us there, whether or not we see him.

Jesus was also God. This means that God loves us enough to have stooped to our station, stepped in person upon the stage where we live our lives, experienced all of what it is to be human. God even knows what it is like to feel abandoned by God. When God says to us, "I know how much this hurts you. I know what you're going through," God speaks the truth. God knows because he has been there himself.

❦ 22.14-15

I am poured out like water;
all my bones are out of joint;
   my heart within my breast is melting wax.
My mouth is dried out like a pot-sherd;
my tongue sticks to the roof of my mouth;
   and you have laid me in the dust of
      the grave.

Rarely have I read a more vivid description of severe illness. I have visited many people who felt as this psalmist felt. One woman I remember especially. Diagnosed with terminal cancer at 42, she experienced all the pains the psalmist mentions. Through it all, she grew more and more serene, often comforting those who had come to comfort her. In the end, when she finally said her good-byes and died, she had given her loved ones a glimpse into her noble soul which she had not granted, perhaps could not have granted, before.

John Donne wrote a series of devotions during a grave illness. He wrote that although God had taken him off his feet, God had not removed him from his foundation, which was God himself; though God had removed his eyesight, yet

God had not removed that light which enabled him to see God himself; though God had weakened his bodily knees, yet God had left him with the knees of his heart, which were bowed to God evermore.

It is good to praise God in pleasant times, but the real saints are those who are able to praise God even when darkness, doubt, and death are advancing.

⧳ 23.1

The LORD is my shepherd;
I shall not be in want.

Modern America is a restless society. People are always on the move, driving for something more or better. For most Americans, material needs are more than met, but the restlessness persists. This suggests that having material things, though undeniably preferable to lacking them, provides little real contentment. I myself have often felt this restlessness in my soul. I have never known real want. My outward circumstances have always been more than comfortable and I have never lacked for anything needed to sustain life. But inwardly I have sometimes experienced a certain longing, nagging doubts, and a suspicion that I lack what really matters. I have wanted to gaze on the face of God and rest in the arms of God, but I could not find God.

King David, presumably the author of this psalm, apparently found what so many modern Americans long for. Thinking of God, he envisioned green pastures, still waters, righteous paths, a table set for a feast, anointing with fragrant oil, an overflowing cup. These seem to have been real experiences for David. David's outward circumstances were often troubled—by temptation, guilt, enemies, the death of a beloved son—but through it all, David found contentment in the arms of God. St. Paul also found it and wrote of it to the Philippians, "I have learned to be content with whatever I have." He wrote these words from a prison cell.

What did David and Paul do that we have not done? I'm not sure, but I believe it has to do with total obedience, holding nothing back, saying yes to God with the whole heart, mind, and soul. I have flirted with that, drawn close but then stepped away. What if I were to draw close and not step away? Would I find what my soul longs for? What holds me back?

○ 23.4c

Your rod and your staff, they comfort me.

This psalm has provided strength and solace to hundreds of generations of Jews and Christians. The shepherd caring for his sheep is one of the tenderest images of God in all of literature.

But being shepherded is not usually a comforting experience. If the shepherd is a figure for God, then the sheep are a figure for human beings. Sheep are stupid animals, who do not recognize danger and often wander into it. If they are to be saved from themselves, they must be protected from their own foolishness and waywardness. The shepherd's rod or staff is a long stick with a crook in the end with which the shepherd reaches out and yanks the sheep by the neck to drag it back to safety. At the moment of the yanking, the sheep surely doesn't entertain congenial thoughts about the shepherd and does not consider the rod and staff a "comfort." The sheep, after all, would not have wandered near the wolf or to the edge of the ravine if it hadn't expected to have a good time there; and even on those occasions when the wolf and ravine cannot be avoided in our lives, most of us do not wish to be yanked back from them by a crook around the neck.

We usually think we know what is best for us and how to extricate ourselves from dangerous or unpleasant situations. We are more interested in pressing our rights, realizing our true selves, kicking up our heels, and taking charge of our lives than in taking directions from the shepherd. Being yanked back or disciplined is a comfort only to those who acknowledge their ignorance and helplessness, who realize they need a shepherd.

ℭℛ 24.1

The earth is the LORD's and all that is in it,
the world and all who dwell therein.

I once visited a remote area in eastern Zimbabwe where little rain falls. My guide pointed to a mountain through which an irrigation channel had been cut. He explained that when they began digging the channel, they prayed first to God, then to their ancestors, then to the mountain: "We ask your pardon, O God, for cutting into the work of your hands. We do it only because we need water to live. We ask your pardon, O ancestors, for disturbing the land where you are buried. We do it only because we need water to live. We ask your pardon, O mountain, for hurting you by cutting into your side. We do it only because we need water to live."

While I thought it strange to pray to ancestors and to a mountain, I was moved by the reverence these African Christians felt for God, those who had come before them, and the natural order. They assumed that all things, past and present, animate and inanimate, are the Lord's and that human beings are charged with the responsibility to care for them. This is a part of stewardship. I had encountered this understanding before in ancient Celtic and native American spirituality. It was with sadness that I thought of attitudes in the West today, where God is often not considered and the natural order is seen as ours to use or dispose of as we will. Something is deeply wrong in a culture that thinks nothing of gouging out pits, mines, quarries, ditches, and landfills. It's not that we should never do such things, but we should do them with reverence and to the glory of God, conscious of our place as part of nature. Too often we construct things which neither glorify God nor provide for the needs of God's creatures.

↳ 24.7,9

Lift up your heads, O gates;
lift them high, O everlasting doors;
and the King of glory shall come in.

These lines apparently comprised a hymn sung at the Jerusalem temple, the gates and the doors being those of the temple. Although the ancient Jews never thought of the Lord's power and presence as confined to the temple on Mount Zion, it was seen as the Lord's home. When we say or sing these lines, we may think of our modern churches as places where the doors must be open to the presence of the Lord. But it is not primarily in buildings that God resides, as Solomon himself acknowledged after erecting the first temple (I Kings 8). We can apply these words in two other, analogous ways as well:

God is present within the community of his people, but he must be invited and expected. I once interviewed to become rector of a parish which hoped some day to construct a new church building. When I asked the warden when they thought that day would come, he said, "We're more interested in building a Christian community. The time for bricks and mortar will come later." I accepted the call to that parish, and the warden was right—I experienced the presence of God in that place, in the faithfulness and warmth of the church community. It was a worshiping community that opened its doors and expected the Lord to enter. The bricks and mortar came later.

God is also present in the heart of every faithful Christian, but he must be invited. I think of the words of the hymn by Georg Weissel: "Fling wide the portals of your heart, make it a temple set apart from earthly use for heaven's employ, adorned with prayer and love and joy."

❧ 25.3

Show me your ways, O LORD,
and teach me your paths.

I often pray verses 3 through 11 of this psalm as a morning devotion. The blending of trust, penitence, humility, and the request for guidance contained in these verses strikes just the right balance to begin a new day.

To learn the ways and paths of the Lord, I begin with the Bible. For me, there is no substitute for daily reading and reflection on the scriptures. I read the scriptures as part of my morning prayer time. This teaches me to think as the biblical authors thought. By reflecting upon events in their lives, the ancient Israelites and early Christians came to understand their relationship to the Lord. They saw how God was working out his purposes in the events of their lives and the world around them. The Bible is the record of those events and of how the Lord used them to disclose his ways to his people and teach them his paths. Through the Bible, we learn to see things as the biblical authors saw them and to discover the hand of the Lord in the events of our lives, as they discovered it in the events of their lives.

The written word, however, is not God's primary communication of his ways and paths; it merely points to it. If we would know the Lord in the fullest and most intimate way, we look not to sacred texts, but to a person disclosed in the texts—we look to Jesus Christ. It is as if God said, "I shall do more than tell you about myself and my hope for your lives. I shall give you more than commandments, more than a book. I shall show you my ways and teach you my paths in person. I will give you an actual demonstration of who I am and what I hope for you. I shall live among you. If you would meet me, meet me where you are."

❧ 25.6

Remember not the sins of my youth and
my transgressions;
remember me according to your love
and for the sake of your goodness, O LORD.

Sins of youth are different from other transgressions. They are often due less to selfish willfulness than to lack of experience in life resulting in ill-informed and headstrong behaviors. Most of us survive the sins of youth, and this psalm suggests that God does not remember them. I like the thought that God does not remember the sins of my youth (though I doubt I shall ever forget them). The transgressions of adulthood, however, are something else. By the time we reach maturity, we should have learned some things about God, ourselves, and human relationships, much of it from reflecting on the consequences of the sins of youth. Adults are held to a higher standard of accountability.

But we are slow learners. We often repeat again and

again the same destructive behaviors that got us into trouble in our youth, some of us persisting in these patterns into old age. That is why it is important to pray daily to be forgiven for our past failures and that we might learn and profit from them in the days to come.

We know that God will remember us—that is not in question. We ask that he remember us not according to his wrath, justified though he might be in doing so, but according to his love; not for the sake of our goodness, shoddy and unreliable as it is, but for the sake of his goodness, strong as granite and deep as the ocean.

ℭ 25.7-9

Gracious and upright is the LORD;
therefore he teaches sinners in his way.
He guides the humble in doing right
and teaches his way to the lowly.
All the paths of the LORD are love and
faithfulness
to those who keep his covenant and
his testimonies.

As we see a diamond differently when it reflects the light from different angles, so we catch a different glimpse of God from each phrase of this short passage. The Lord is gracious. The Lord is upright. The Lord is loving. The Lord is faithful. Each attribution points to a different aspect of God's character, but they can become platitudes if we repeat them cursorily and without thinking about them.

It is well to remember that although these divine attributes are not in question, they don't necessarily make a difference in our lives, and for many, it may as well not be so. The flip side of the Lord's dependable goodness is our humility and obedience. The Lord teaches sinners in his way, but we must be willing to learn. The guidance and teaching of the Lord are there for all to see, in the Bible and most of all in the person of Jesus Christ, but it is only the humble and the lowly who are actually guided and taught. The proud and the mighty may as well have no eyes, for they do not see. All the paths of the Lord are love and faithfulness, and the invitation to travel down those paths is extended to all, but if you would journey down those paths, you must keep his commandments and his testimonies. We are free to choose and the Lord will not compel us to make the right choice.

ॐ 26.2-3

Test me, O LORD, and try me;
examine my heart and my mind.
For your love is before my eyes;
I have walked faithfully with you.

It takes a lot of nerve to pray a prayer like that. It isn't necessary, of course, to invite God to examine our hearts and minds, because God knows quite well what is there, whether we invite him to take a look or not. It's just that we know what's there as well, and while it isn't all foul and peevish, much of it is. If I could, I'd choose not to place my heart and mind under the divine microscope. Or failing that, I'd at least ask for time to launder my heart and mind before submitting them to examination.

This psalmist was often at church. He makes several references to his churchgoing ways. There are three possibilities here. First, the psalmist might, just possibly, have been as pure as he said he was. I doubt it, but if so, he was probably lonely and disliked. That's what usually happens to the radically faithful. People resent them. Second, he may have been blind to his own sins and failures. That's more likely, and if that was the case, his self-righteous posturing surely made him insufferable, and I hope this psalm wasn't the last thing he wrote, because he had a lot of growing to do before reaching spiritual maturity. Third, he may have been referring to himself as seen in the eyes of a forgiving God, cleansed and purified at God's initiative. If that was the case, then the psalmist had progressed far in his journey into the arms of God, and his words can serve for us as a lamp along the way.

One thing have I asked of the LORD;
one thing I seek;
      that I may dwell in the house of the LORD
            all the days of my life;
To behold the fair beauty of the LORD
      and to seek him in his temple.

Rudolf Otto wrote of the *mysterium tremendum,* that quality of God which stupefies and overwhelms—the absolute otherness and power of God. This psalm celebrates another divine quality of which Otto wrote and which often accompanies the *mysterium tremendum,* the quality of *fascinans.* Although baffled by divine mystery and subdued by divine power, we also find God alluring, attractive, beautiful; we are irresistibly drawn to God. There is, as Augustine said, a God-shaped hole within us that remains a painful emptiness until it is filled, and it can only be filled with the one for whom it was made, and who made it. God made us for himself, and we long for God like aliens longing for a homeland—we are *fascinated* by God.

The request to dwell in the Lord's house and to behold the Lord's beauty are two of many expressions of *fascinans* found in this psalm. The psalm pleads for, then confidently celebrates, a closeness, a tender familiarity that transcends mystery and power. The psalmist wants to dwell in the house of the Lord because persons who dwell in the same house know one another intimately; they share secrets.

The psalmist could not have imagined the lengths to

which God would go to answer his request for a relation of tender intimacy. Centuries later, God set aside his mystery and power to enter the world in person, to make the world itself his home. God may now be known anywhere. His dwelling place is with his people, wherever we are and whatever we do.

☙ 27.11

You speak in my heart and say, "Seek my face."
Your face, LORD, will I seek.

This verse points to one of the most profound paradoxes of the spiritual life. Many people today experience a deep spiritual hunger. They may not trust institutional religion, and traditional religious language may make them squirm. But they are quick to say they seek meaning in their lives, which is the same thing as seeking God. Spirituality is the word often used to refer to this hunger. Even those who don't want to be "religious" want to be "spiritual." And so they search, many of them unsure where to look or even what they're looking for. Even in the churches, many people feel this hunger and don't know how to satisfy it.

The paradox is that if you are searching for God and even if you don't know it's God you are searching for, God is already present in your life. If God were not there, you would not be moved to search for him. This became clear to me many years ago when, as a recovering alcoholic, I discovered the presence and power of God in my life in a way I had not anticipated. When I entered recovery, I merely wanted to stop drinking. I had no idea that I would come to know God in the process. Years later, when I looked back on the time of my active drinking and the fear and isolation it inflicted upon me, I began to see that the hand of God had been working in my soul even before I consciously turned to him. "Twas grace that taught my heart to fear," as the hymn says.

The pain, emptiness, or longing that drives you to search for God is actually God already moving in your soul, trying to get your attention. When you are finally able to acknowledge the presence and power of God in your life, he may say to you, "At last you've noticed! I've been with you all along, waiting for this moment!"

☙ 27.18

O tarry and await the LORD's pleasure;
be strong, and he shall comfort your heart;
wait patiently for the LORD.

There is a fitful, hurried kind of waiting. We wait for a long light to turn green; we wait for the clerk at the supermarket to ring up groceries; we fidget in the waiting room of the doctor's office. We'd rather be moving, doing something, going somewhere. We have a sense that we're wasting time.

This psalm suggests a different kind of waiting. Those who tarry or wait patiently are not in a hurry; they do not steal glances at their watches; they are unconcerned about the passage of time. When we wait for the Lord, it is this second kind of waiting.

Years ago, I grandly undertook to become a spiritual master by reading all the spiritual classics I could find. I rushed through them, polishing them off by the dozens, from the early church fathers up through the modern era. My shelf of finished books overflowed onto a second and then a third shelf. But I hardly remembered anything I had read, and I certainly didn't become a spiritual master. My goal, I later realized, had not been to commune with God, still less to invite God to challenge and change me, but to finish the books so that I could refer to them in sermons and conversations, impressing others with my learning. It was an exercise in vanity.

I still read spiritual books. But now I linger over a single page, or even a single sentence. It may take me months to complete a book, and sometimes I don't complete it. It doesn't matter. The important thing is not how many books I read, but the quiet, unhurried moments I spend tarrying—questioning, musing, laughing—with the Lord.

℘ 28.1

O LORD, I call to you;
my Rock, do not be deaf to my cry;
lest, if you do not hear me,
I become like those who go down to the Pit.

This psalm is like a piece of music that modulates into different keys. The psalm has three keys. It begins with a desperate plea not to be forgotten, then asks that the psalmist's enemies be given what they deserve, then concludes with words of thanksgiving, joy, and trust. The first two keys seem related; the third is quite different and may have been written at a later time, when the troubles giving rise to the earlier verses had been happily resolved.

I read the latter verses in the light of the opening plea of desperation. The psalmist fears that God may not hear his cry. Why? Because he has been defeated at every turn? Because he has sought God's attention but gotten nothing but silence? Because he has done something that he fears may cause God to reject him? Because the voices of those who go down to "the Pit" cannot reach God? Because he has lost faith in God altogether? It is a short step from this sort of hopeless self-obsession to the focusing of one's anger on others who have wronged us or who we imagine have wronged us, which we see in verses 3 to 6 of this psalm—"My problems are their fault and they should get what they deserve!"

Not knowing the details of the psalmist's pain, we cannot know how it was resolved, but it is well to remember that this psalm ends on a note of affirmation. We may feel desolate and fear that God has turned his back on us forever, but God does not forget us.

ᐧᐧ 29.1

Ascribe to the LORD, you gods,
   ascribe to the LORD glory and strength.

What gods?

If we take the word "god" to refer only to the supreme Creator of the universe, then it's hard to imagine how there could be more than one. But perhaps it refers to lesser heavenly beings. This verse introduces a psalm in which thunder, lightening, heavy wind, crashing ocean waves, and perhaps earthquakes suggest "the voice of the Lord." I envision the psalmist sitting somewhere amidst the storm, wind, and waves, listening to the sounds of power and might all around him. These sounds suggest to him the glory of God, and as they lift his imagination to celestial realms, his mind hears heavenly voices joining that chorus of earthly sounds around the throne where the Lord sits, reigning over all.

For some modern people, whose lives are far removed from the events of nature and who attribute storm, wind, and waves to natural causes, these things might not be so suggestive of heavenly power as they were to the psalmist. But we are more aware than the psalmist of the vast expanses of outer space and the infinitesimal wonders of subatomic particles. For us, it is perhaps these things that suggest heavenly voices glorifying God.

But are there such heavenly voices? I'll be surprised if the answer is no. The Bible makes reference to many heavenly beings, from angels and archangels to cherubim and seraphim. I doubt that this is merely colorful verbiage. Surely God, the Creator of all that is, did not limit himself to what human beings can see and touch and feel. Why would God have done that when so many other imaginative and winsome possibilities must have come to his mind as well? We are, I suspect, but one order of being, among a vast array of fellow creatures whose nature and existence we could not grasp even if we met them face to face, which perhaps we have and don't know it.

ᐊᕈ 29.9

And in the temple of the L<small>ORD</small>
all are crying, "Glory!"

The context of this verse suggests that the psalmist is not thinking of an earthly temple, but of a heavenly one. Who or what might be included in this "all" who are crying "Glory" in heaven?

Heavenly beings, presumably. The Bible refers to many such beings, but apart from the occasional mystical encounter, we have little experience of them, and even those few experiences are hard to understand and account for. In this life we can see but dim reflections of that heavenly temple and hear only faint echos of the voices there crying "Glory!"

But I expect earthly creatures are part of that heavenly chorus as well, even creatures with which we are so familiar that we hardly give them a thought. The common images of heaven, with golden streets and pearly gates, though biblical in origin, leave me cold. I prefer to imagine a scene where heavenly creatures praise God in concert with creatures familiar to me from earth—dragonflies, river otters, electric eels, oak trees, nettles, minerals, mountains, streams, skies, bogs, winds, and sunbeams. I also envision planets, galaxies, subatomic particles, time warps and black holes, the bizarre creatures of relativity and quantum mechanics joining the chorus. I imagine human expressions—poems, symphonies, sculptures, and prayers, spoken from churches and temples, from hospital rooms, from dungeons and concentration camps, all joining their voices in heavenly praise. I imagine the great persons of history, together with the myriads of little persons lost in history, in a single chorus of all races, religions, temperaments, and times. God grant that someday I may add my voice to that heavenly chorus, that I too may cry "Glory!" in the temple of the Lord. Meanwhile, I sing with the saints on earth as we wait "till in heaven we take our place, till we cast our crowns before thee, lost in wonder, love, and praise."

℘ 30.6

Weeping may spend the night,
but joy comes in the morning.

It would be presumptuous of me to pretend to be an expert on weeping. My life has been largely a happy one and I rarely shed tears, in the middle of the night or at any other time. When I consider what others have experienced, I realize I've been spared many griefs. But my troubles have tripped me up and thrown me down on occasion, leading me to feel like crying even when I could not summon actual tears. The soul sometimes weeps dry tears. I have wept in the middle of the night—over the death of my father, the collapse of my sense of who I was, the loss of my faith, the fear that life was a cruel joke and that nothing mattered at all. Sometimes I weep still.

This weeping has lasted in some cases for a long time, even several years. But I continue to pray during those times. It seems that prayer is the only thing I can do, even when I have lost any sense of the reality of the God to whom I address my prayers. And so I pray, sometimes without feeling, without belief, without conviction, perhaps from mere habit, out of boredom and the lack of energy to do anything else.

Does the mere act of continuing to pray, listless though my prayers may be, hasten the dawn, or would the dawn come in any case? I don't know and I don't have to know. I doubt that God waits for our prayers before acting, but I suspect our praying helps to open us to God's influence when we've been shriveled or imprisoned by troubles and that it contributes in some way to bringing our weeping to an end. Whatever the reason, morning breaks and joy comes again to us. Now when I find myself weeping in the night, I try to remember that "weeping may spend the night, but joy comes in the morning."

I am forgotten like a dead man, out of mind;
I am as useless as a broken pot.

Miss Charlotte Elliott was the invalid sister of a clergyman. She lived with her brother in Brighton, England, where he was vicar of the local Anglican parish in 1835. The vicarage was located adjacent to the church. One afternoon Miss Elliott's brother and his parishioners were busily preparing for a bazaar to be held on the church grounds to benefit a school for the daughters of poor clergymen which the parish operated. Miss Elliott lay in her bed, unable to render any assistance. Through her open bedroom window, she heard the others at work in the yard below. She felt worthless, "useless as a broken pot." It was at this time that she wrote the beloved hymn, "Just as I am."

I have met many people who felt worthless and have on occasion felt worthless myself. Sometimes, as in Miss Elliott's case, the feeling results from the inability to do what others do. Often it results from having been abused, belittled, overlooked, or taken for granted by those from whom we sought love, respect, or recognition. Whatever its source, the feeling of worthlessness can paralyze the soul.

Miss Elliott's great hymn contains a profound antidote to the feeling of worthlessness. Each stanza begins with the words "Just as I am," affirming that however weak, guilty, confused, or doubtful we may be, God will receive, pardon, cleanse, and relieve us. The concluding words of each stanza are also essential: "I come." To claim that promise, we come to Jesus, open ourselves to him who is constantly seeking us out and bidding us "Come!" When we have received Jesus into our hearts, we will no longer be just as we were, but splendidly transformed.

℘ 32.10

Do not be like horse or mule, which have no understanding;
who must be fitted with bit and bridle,
or else they will not stay near you.

When the Bible compares humankind to an animal, the comparison is usually to sheep and the thrust of the comparison typically is that "all we like sheep have gone astray" and need a shepherd to pull or bring us home again. Here, though, we are warned not to be "horsy" or "mulish." The thrust of the horse and mule comparison is similar to the more familiar one of the sheep, but it has a slightly different twist.

Sheep are left free to roam where they wish. They typically scatter over a hillside like marbles dropped onto a tile floor. When the sheep wander too far, the shepherd (or a sheepdog) rounds them up and brings them back. Horses and mules, however, do not roam. They are fenced in. Then, when needed for plowing, pulling a load, or another task, they are taken out of the corral and fitted with a bit and bridle to control or channel their behavior. Horses and mules are disciplined, as it were, *before* they wander off.

So are we more like sheep or more like horses and mules? Does God give us free rein, then rescue us from the troubles we create for ourselves, or does he restrain us before the fact? I don't know. If my experience is any indication, it's some of both. At times I've wandered off willfully and gotten myself into a mess. I required rescuing—and God rescued me, usually by means of some unexpected agent. At other times, routes that might have landed me in trouble were closed to me before I could choose to travel down them. But it doesn't matter in the end. The important thing is to attend to the voice of the Lord so that we grow in grace until we willingly become all the Lord means us to be. Then no discipline, before or after the fact, will be needed.

ᴑᴙ 33:2-3

Praise the LORD with the harp;
play to him upon the psaltery and lyre.
Sing for him a new song;
sound a fanfare with all your skill upon
the trumpet.

Souls that are harried and hurried need to be slowed down—and music is often the answer. When I sing a classic Christian hymn, my soul pauses. When I play Chopin or Schumann on the piano, or listen to a Mozart symphony or a requiem mass, my soul stops to listen. The first time I heard Charles Wesley's "Love divine, all loves excelling" sung to the tune Blaenwern, which is little known in America, I was in Britain driving my car and could not continue. I pulled off the road to listen. Years later I heard a choir of 70 seminarians in Nigeria sing it again and was once again stopped in my tracks. Musical tastes differ, but I expect there is a musical respite for every busy soul willing to stop dashing and darting about long enough to sing, play, or listen.

Non-musical sounds also slow down my soul. I often pray on my porch, where whippoorwills, mockingbirds, crickets, and breezes in the trees speak to me of God. So, too, do human sounds such as cars passing, airplanes overhead, lawnmowers, mothers yelling down the street for their children, children yelling for their puppies, sirens and bells, and basketballs hitting the pavement of a neighbor's driveway. I often listen patiently to these sounds and envision God in the hearts of those producing the sounds.

A new hymn, "Earth and all stars," by Herbert Brokering, calls upon engines and steel, pounding hammers, boiling test-tubes, and cheering crowds to join in singing for the Lord a new song. Could we even learn to listen to cash registers, jet airplanes, screeching tires, ringing telephones, and honking horns as sounds of praise? Inspiring as sacred music can be, do we sometimes overlook the messages of God's presence to be heard in common, everyday sounds?

℞ 33.11

But the LORD's will stands fast for ever,
and the designs of his heart from age to age.

"The Lord's will" can seem a heavy phrase, suggesting some plan for our lives which we cannot know, conceived in the inscrutable mind of God, unchangeable and lasting forever. More than once I have prayed for guidance—"Just a hint of direction, please, Lord!"—when facing an important decision, but God's will for me was usually no clearer after my praying than before.

Occasionally, however, I've been sure of God's will (or thought I was). Then I faced a different task—trying to pump myself up with enough courage, strength, commitment, faith, or whatever, to go out and do it. I don't know which made me feel worse—not knowing God's will for me, or knowing it and failing to do it. Either way, God's will felt like a burden I couldn't shake off; either way, I lost.

The second part of this verse suggests a different understanding of God's will. Perhaps it is a matter of the heart, less something God wants us to do than a relationship with us that God longs for. Maybe it's like a marriage—the most splendid thing about my wife isn't what she does for me (though I appreciate that), but the fact that she loves me. Perhaps God is less concerned about where we live and work, with whom we associate, what we do and say, our outward circumstances, than about the orientation of our hearts. Perhaps his deepest desire is that we simply enjoy the pleasure of his company and invite him to enjoy the pleasure of ours. Perhaps the phrase "the will of God," so often heard as a heavy demand or expectation laid on us by an uncompromising and omnipotent deity, is really just God's longing to relax and be at ease with us.

℘ 34.1a

I will bless the LORD at all times.

All times? Times come and go. Circumstances and relationships come and go. Hopes, fears, and moods come and go. We cannot be singing hymns, reciting psalms, extolling the name of the Lord all the time. We cannot even be thinking about the Lord all the time. Sometimes we must vacuum floors, pay bills, do homework, buy groceries, mow grass, change diapers, fix things.

If we are to bless the Lord at all times, it must mean we are to bless him even when we're thinking about something else. There are, of course, some things we must discipline ourselves not to think about, such as the lust for revenge, envy of others, and prurient images. It is impossible to bless the Lord when the mind is occupied with thoughts antithetic to the Lord.

But if we intentionally give every moment to the Lord, seeking his guidance, blessing, and discipline in all things, and asking that he enable us to amend our lives where necessary, we become so permeated with the mind of God that we bless him unconsciously, whatever we're thinking about. Our very breath and heartbeat become acts of praise.

The 17th century Discalced Carmelite known as Brother Lawrence worked in a monastery kitchen most of his life. "I possess God as peacefully in the bustle of my kitchen, where sometimes several people are asking me for different things at the same time, as I do upon my knees before the Blessed Sacrament," he wrote. "I turn my little omelette in the pan for the love of God." Brother Lawrence called this "the practice of the presence of God." It stems from the heart, he said, not from outward observances. To bless the Lord at all times is to allow our hearts and minds to be so transformed that Christ himself lives in us. We become miniature Christs. Every thought, every word, every deed, every priority, every decision is an act of Christlike obedience. It is no longer we who do it, but Christ in us.

℞ 34.8a

Taste and see that the LORD is good.

Can we really taste and see the Lord's goodness, or is that just a quaint metaphor? All things disclose something of their Maker. Consider what our senses suggest about God:

Taste: Ripe mangoes pulled from the tree, cold spring water, sharp cheddar cheese, coconut rind, the first cup of coffee in the morning, Bermuda onions in a turbulent salad, a warm chocolate chip cookie, Jesus extending himself to you in bread and wine, an ice cream cone shared with a child.

Sight: Shimmering shades of gray in full moonlight, soft silver circles around that moon on a moist night, undulating water ripples, speckled pebbles on a Michigan beach, pelicans in flight, live oak trees, mountains, seas, dunes, rivers, canyons, plains, deserts, tundras, bogs, cliffs, glades—and the shape and smile of the one you love.

Hearing: Wind in the leaves, rustling feet in the leaves after they fall, the mockingbird and those he mocks, church bells in the distance, raindrops falling from branches after a storm, fire crackling on the hearth, a Beethoven concerto, a sharp line drive, thunder clapping, waves crashing, crickets chirping, newborns crying, the words "I love you and I always will." And silence.

Smell: Steely air in your lungs on a winter day, honeysuckle, fresh mown grass, bread in the oven, the pages of a new book, a salt sea breeze, orange groves, coffee perking, camellia blossoms.

Touch: Rough tree bark, plush moss beneath moist ferns, bare feet on dewy grass, soft earth at planting time, snowflakes on your cheek, spring sunshine warming your bones, the splash of baptism on your head, a child folded in your arms, yourself folded in the arms of another.

These are the notes of the symphony of God. What do they tell us of their composer? And how best might we dance in response to One who has shared such music with us?

ℜ 35.1

Fight those who fight me, O LORD;
attack those who are attacking me.

This psalmist sees himself as a victim and his mind revolves around themes such as the maliciousness of others, his own innocence, and the glee he will feel when the Lord pays his enemies back, makes their way "dark and slippery."

I find this psalm tedious. It's self-righteousness, bent on getting even, quickly wears thin for me. We cannot know the circumstances which gave rise to such feelings, but the psalmist clearly has other people in mind. It is possible he has been truly wronged. It is also possible he has blown his afflictions out of proportion in his mind, or possibly even concocted them out of his imagination. The one thing we can say for certain is that the psalmist is consumed by a sour, inward-looking self-righteous vengefulness. Every one of us has known these feelings occasionally, some of us often, and we all must do battle with them. That they find such unrestrained expression in this and other psalms is one of the things that makes the Psalms such an easy collection of songs to claim as our own—they are very human.

Nigerian novelist and Nobel laureate Wole Soyinka has written an eloquent account of his incarceration, isolation, and torture by the military dictatorship of his country in the late 1960s, entitled *The Man Died*. Demeaning and cruel though his treatment was, Soyinka focuses primarily on the ways he defended himself during his confinement against self-pity, anger, boredom, vengefulness, and despair. Although the psalmist may not realize it, when he asks the Lord to fight his enemies, the primary battleground may be not the world outside him, but the world inside him.

ೞ 36.9b

In your light we see light.

As a young man, I wondered about the existence of God. I wanted to believe in God, but my mind kept objecting. I recall deciding one day to investigate the matter until I found the answer. I read lots of books on philosophy and theology, weighing every bit of the evidence for and against the existence of God.

I finally realized I would never find the answer. The more theories I poured into my head, the more confounded I became. I further realized that I didn't even know who or what this God was, much less whether he (she? it? they?) existed. It dawned on me that ignorance was not a condition I would overcome, try as I might, but my normal (God-given?) state of being. I would remain ignorant, and someday I would die, still ignorant. I could either fight it, or I could accept it and follow what small glimmers of light I occasionally saw. I chose to accept my ignorance and follow the glimmers.

A remarkable thing happened. I came to experience a contentment I had not known before, a security like that of a child in its mother's arms. My mind still objects, but intellectual proofs and disproofs no longer seem important. I remembered a quotation from St. Anselm which I had come across while reading theology years earlier: "I believe that I may know." I didn't understand it at the time, but now I do. I had wanted to know in order that I might believe. It happens the other way around.

℘ 37.4

Take delight in the LORD,
and he shall give you your heart's desire.

Many things delight me: I delight in my wife, in taking walks with her in the park and in lying in her arms in the early morning. I delight in watching my three sons create lives for themselves, building upon and surpassing what I taught them as children. Old friendships delight me, as does the prospect of new ones. I love running two miles every day. The music of Beethoven and Brahms and Chopin charms me. I delight in reading challenging books and the morning newspaper. Traveling to new places and gaining new experiences makes me happy. And I love my quiet time with God every day. All these are good and healthy delights, if not identical to delighting in God, then surely consistent with it. But I have also delighted in things false and dangerous, such as senseless ambition, insisting on my own opinion or wishes, and pretending to be what I am not. I sometimes suspect that vain delights motivate even the good that I do.

Lord, have I ever truly delighted in you? Have I ever loved you purely for the goodness and beauty that is yourself? Have I ever really known you, Lord? There have been moments when I sensed a closeness to you, felt a spiritual glow or buzz, wanted to dance before you as David danced. But what was it about such moments that delighted me, Lord? Could it have been something other than yourself that gave me pleasure? I know that to gain even the most noble of delights is to gain nothing if I lack you. To those who delight in you, Lord, and not in some lesser thing, you have promised to grant their heart's desire, which is to grant them yourself, to come to them to heal, restore, and embrace them. Grant, O Lord, that perceiving you in all pleasures, I may delight in you with a pure and perpetual passion. So knit my heart to you, so possess my will, so fill my thoughts and my desires, that I may be wholly yours, loving you in all things and above all things. Then I shall obtain your promises, which exceed all that I can desire.

Refrain from anger, leave rage alone;
do not fret yourself; it leads only to evil.

There is a place for anger. Even Jesus was angry—but not at the sorts of things that usually make us angry. When Jesus became angry, it was because of the injustice, hypocrisy, and falsehood he saw all around him. He railed at the scribes and Pharisees and threw the money changers out of the temple, letting his anger vent. This was anger on behalf of others. But when betrayed, arrested, and killed, he accepted it with apparent calm.

Most of our anger arises from injured pride, jealousy, and self-pity. We tell ourselves that our abilities and insight exceed those of our peers, that we have received less than our due, that another's promotion or good fortune should have been ours, that life has been unfair to us. Then we hold onto these thoughts, repeating and refining them in our minds, until they become demons that consume our souls. Such anger is typical of persons suffering from compulsions and addictions, whether chemical or otherwise. Compulsive and addicted people must have their way, and when they don't get it, anger wells up.

Consider the example of Jesus. When he threw the moneychangers out of the temple, his outburst had nothing to do with pride, jealousy, or self-pity, but with a violation of a holy place. And when it was over, it was over—Jesus did not nurse his anger. He was able to refrain from anger because he neither envied nor judged others, and was content, even in the most adverse circumstances. He had fully surrendered his will to God and knew how to trust God in all things. When we learn to do the same, we too will be content in all things.

℘ 37.19a,21a

The LORD cares for the lives of the godly....
As for the wicked, they shall perish.

This long psalm consists largely of a string of assertions that the Lord will give those who trust him whatever they want and that the wicked will be slapped with the punishment they deserve. The righteous will "possess the land" while the wicked "vanish like smoke." Real soon. Just you wait and see.

Whom is the psalmist trying to convince? The Bible is inconsistent on this question. The Book of Job seems to say one thing, Ecclesiastes another, and Proverbs yet another. The Psalms give lots of answers. And then there's the New Testament, with its central tale of an innocent person being executed for a crime he didn't commit. I find the attitude of this psalm hard to take, not merely because the Bible offers other perspectives on what happens to good and bad people, but also because the psalm doesn't jive with what I see happening around me. Maybe in the next life God will even the score, but he doesn't seem to do it in this life, at least not always, not reliably, not that I can see. And I'm not even sure I want the score evened—I'd rather see the wicked forgiven and changed, but that doesn't always happen, either.

Why God allows evil to flourish is a question that has troubled philosophers and theologians, to say nothing of ordinary people, for thousands of years. We are not likely to answer it. The question we need to ask is not why God allows evil, but how we will live in a world where injustice abounds. If we allow ourselves to be consumed by anger or defeated by pessimism, no one is the better—but our peace of mind vanishes and our health erodes. The better course is to accept that we live in an imperfect and confounding world and are ourselves imperfect and confounding. Then we can do our part to make the world a better place, and ourselves better inhabitants and stewards of it.

❧ 38.1-2

O Lᴏʀᴅ, do not rebuke me in your anger;
do not punish me in your wrath.
For your arrows have already pierced me,
and your hand presses hard upon me.

The opening verse of this psalm is the same as that with which Psalm 6 opens, and while the two psalms are similar in many ways (possibly by the same author?), this psalm is darker, lacking the note of affirmation with which Psalm 6 concludes. Here we have one long, unrelieved, desperate cry. And as if the psalmist's pain, so graphically described, weren't bad enough, he seems convinced that God has intentionally inflicted it upon him as an act of wrath. The hand of

God, elsewhere an image of tender guidance and love, here becomes a fist that grips, squeezes, clutches, bruises, beats.

Does God really treat people that way, or is the psalmist mistaken about God's role in his suffering? I believe the psalmist is mistaken, although it is tempting, when we are beaten down by adversity, to think that God has done it to us. Like the psalmist, many an oppressed person has, rightly or wrongly, looked to God as the author of his misery.

An African acquaintance said to me, not long after the terrorist attacks of September 11, 2001, "Don't you think God is punishing America for the evil things America represents in the world?" I said I did not believe that. "America is not an evil country," I said, "at least no more evil than any other country, although it is more powerful than other countries and it could use its power more fairly and humanely. But even if America were the very definition of evil, I don't believe God bashes people, even wicked people. God has structured the world in such a way that evil carries a price, but it isn't as simple as you would have it. Sometimes the price is paid by the guilty, sometimes by the innocent, sometimes even by God himself."

C∂ 39.5

LORD, let me know my end and the number
of my days,
so that I may know how short my life is.

This is not a request I would make of God. I do not wish to
know the number of my days. Let me arise each morning
assuming that I shall live another day, and let me lie down
each night assuming that I shall arise in the morning.

I do, however, ask that I may be given the grace and
wisdom to live each day *as if* I knew it were my last. As I
write these words, one of my oldest and best friends has just
been diagnosed with cancer and told he has little chance
of living more than a year. He tells me that he suddenly
regards each moment as precious. His priorities have been
transformed. Things which seemed unimportant and which
he had postponed to an undetermined later time have now
become paramount, while other things he had deemed
important have receded into insignificance. He tells me that
he would have done many things differently if he had always
considered that his days were numbered.

Our days are numbered—it is just that we do not know
their number. When I consider my life in this way, some
things become less important—how much money I make,
what other people think of me, and whether I get my way.
My relationships with God and the people nearest to me,
relaxing and enjoying the moment, sharing my goods
with others, and the things that stir my soul become more
important.

ℭ 39.12b

Like a moth you eat away all that is dear to us;
truly, everyone is but a puff of wind.

The scriptures contain many images for God drawn from daily life, but few are more unexpected or unsettling as this image of God as a moth. The best known reference to a moth in scripture comes from the Sermon on the Mount, where Jesus says, "Do not lay up for yourselves treasures on earth, where moth and rust consume and where thieves break in and steal, but lay up for yourselves treasures in heaven." (Mt. 6.19) The psalmist seems to suggest not only that our earthly treasures are eaten by the moth, but that the moth is God! Nor is he the only biblical author to compare God to a moth. The prophet Hosea has the Lord saying that he will be like a moth and like dry rot to his people (Hos. 5:12).

I do not believe that God destroys things we hold dear, still less that God "eats away" at them. But...

When we devote our lives to accumulating and holding onto things, whether tangible things such as money and possessions or intangible things such as power, reputation, and the pursuit of pleasure, we are not the consumers, but the consumed. This is the nature of obsession or addiction. It has been my experience that when I begin to be consumed by things, something or someone consumes the things, and I lose them. I feel cheated, frightened, stupid, and angry. Then and only then do I notice God and turn to God. Could it be that in some sense God himself consumes the things that keep me from him in order that I may be driven to my knees and into his arms?

ℰ 40.1

I waited patiently upon the LORD;
  he stooped to me and heard my cry.

Several years ago, I sought guidance about whether to remain in my job or seek a new position. I had come to feel oppressed in the job I then held, but I was willing to remain in it if that was God's will. I went off to a monastery for a week where I prayed to discern God's will. "I'm confused!" I shouted at God. "Do you want me to remain where I am or go somewhere else? Just tell me what you want of me and I'll do it—*just tell me!*" But God was silent. "Where are you when I need you?" I bellowed.

Finally, I heard a voice in the back of my head, saying, "Do you trust me, or don't you? If you don't, then quit saying you do. If you do, then act like it. Relax. Return to your present job. Do the best you can tomorrow. Then do the best you can the next day, and the day after that. I have something in mind for you down the road. I know what it is and I'm the only one who knows. All you need to know is that I'm God and that I'm in charge."

God did indeed have something in mind for me, something I couldn't have foreseen or caused to come about if I had tried. It could only have come to pass by my waiting for God to do what God would do. But why does God require us to wait? Because it teaches us who's in charge? Because it cultivates the virtue of patience? Because waiting enables us to notice what we wouldn't notice if we were always rushing into the future? Because waiting teaches us that we don't need what we think we need? Because God's time just isn't our time? I often recall that voice: "All you need to know is that I'm God and I'm in charge."

❧ 41.11-12

By this I know you are pleased with me,
that my enemy does not triumph over me.
In my integrity you hold me fast,
and shall set me before your face for ever.

Here is another psalm, one of two dozen or so in the Psalter, that focuses on the psalmist's enemies and his feelings towards them. It contains a breadth and scope of sentiments not always found in these psalms. This psalmist gives full expression to the range of his feelings. He begins with a concern for others in need, and it isn't until a few verses later that we learn of his own troubles. There is an admission of the psalmist's guilt in verse 4, balanced by a claim of innocence in verse 12—an apparent inconsistency not uncommon among people facing opposition or betrayal. The psalmist quotes his enemies (he seems to know them very well) and expresses a desire for vengeance, but not until verse 10, and then only briefly. Human and understandable though that sentiment is, he does not dwell on it and lets it pass.

In the end, the psalmist expresses confidence that, scorned as he may be by former friends turned enemies, the Lord is for him, not against him. He even says that the Lord is *pleased* with him. Such an assertion might denote spiritual pride elsewhere, coming from someone else. But the rest of this psalm suggests another meaning. Here it seems to be more a statement about the Lord than about the psalmist. The point is that the Lord takes pleasure in his people, not that the psalmist is the one who gives the Lord pleasure. In this psalm, we see someone struggling with a potentially devastating experience, betrayal by former friends, with honesty, maturity, faith, and grace.

Book Two

☙

Psalms 42 through 72

෫ 42.6,14; 43.5

Why are you so full of heaviness, O my soul?
and why are you so disquieted within me?

Years ago, I experienced an extended time of what I now perceive to have been sloth, *accedie*. My soul had grown shriveled and numb. I frequently awoke in the middle of the night, tense and anxious. When I couldn't sleep, I often read the Psalms. Time and again I turned to these two psalms, and in particular to this reiterated verse. I see the answer to the rhetorical question posed in this verse more clearly now than I saw it then. If I could have given my soul an honest answer in those days, it would have been something like this:

"Why are you so full of heaviness? Why are you so disquieted? Because you have been stepped on, rolled over, and treated like a thing, a function, a role, rather than a person. You've been abused. Some key people in your life have cared only about what you could do for them, not about you. That makes for a heavy, disquieted soul.

"But that's not all. What was done to you, you have also done to others. You have stepped on others, rolled over others, and treated other people like things, functions, roles, rather than as persons. You have abused others. You have judged them because they did not conform to your image of Christian discipleship. You have been full of answers, even to questions no one was asking, and you have grasped for control, even when no one was competing against you for it. You need to confess the sin in yourself."

I did not acknowledge my part in the heaviness that weighed down my soul for a long time. When I finally did, the weight began to lift and I felt free again.

☙ 42.10-11

The LORD grants his loving-kindness in the
daytime;
in the night season his song is with me,
a prayer to the God of my life.
I will say to the God of my strength,
"Why have you forgotten me?
and why do I go so heavily while the enemy
oppresses me?"

This psalmist points to something that surprises many who have recently come to the Lord—the ups and downs, the ins and outs, the hot and cold quality of the spiritual life. New Christians often expect that the glow they feel upon their conversion will remain with them always. They may even think that's what Christian faith is all about. When the glow fades, the tide goes out, and God seems to withdraw, they are surprised and often disillusioned. But this is a natural, normal part of Christian growth.

This psalm comes from a "dry" time in the psalmist's life. His soul is heavy. The psalmist does three things that anyone experiencing such a dry period might be wise to do:

First, he does not pretend to be what he isn't, but pours out his soul, doubts and all, in these plaintive verses. Writing down such thoughts gets them out of our hearts and onto the paper, which often diminishes their power over us.

Second, he remembers a brighter, lighter time when he not only felt the presence of God, but even led the faithful in worship. He draws strength from these memories and the knowledge, probably gained through experience, that in time, the tide will come in again and the darkness will pass.

Third, he reminds himself that even in the night season, his time of darkness and confusion, even when it feels that God is absent or has abandoned him, "his song is with me."

☙ 43.3-4

Send out your light and your truth,
that they may lead me,
and bring me to your holy hill
and to your dwelling;
That I may go to the altar of God,
to the God of my joy and gladness;
and on the harp I will give thanks to you,
O God my God.

This psalm and the one before it (the two are actually a single hymn) vividly describe a crisis in faith. His faith is very important to the psalmist. He remembers when he sang songs of praise and thanksgiving, leading the people in worship. But now his sense of God's presence in his life has dried up. His soul is heavy; his bones are broken. Ungodly people have conspired against him. He feels forgotten by God and he thirsts for God's return. "Why have you forgotten me? Where are you?" he asks of God. In these two verses, the psalmist begs God to lead him back to the temple, back to the altar, where he once led worship and where he hopes he might again serve his Lord with a voice of praise and thanksgiving.

Western culture as a whole may be suffering from a similar sense of divine abandonment. It is certain that many individuals do. We remember or have heard of a time when the sense of God's presence and power in human life was assumed. Perhaps there was a time in our own lives when we assumed God's presence and power, but now the skies appear dark or empty. Meaning and structure and purpose have been clouded over and we now see only gray shadows. These two verses are a prayer for such a time, that God will take the initiative to send out his light and his truth to lead us back to him again, to the home we remember and to which we long to return.

❧ 44.1

We have heard with our ears, O God,
our forefathers have told us,
the deeds you did in their days,
in the days of old.

Across the street from the house in which I grew up lived my mother's parents, and next door to us lived my father's parents. As child, I thought everyone grew up with six forebears within earshot. All these people were eager to teach me the deeds God had done "in the days of old." This included not only what God had done in their lives, but what God had done in the lives of Bible characters and of Christians in ages long past. I grew up knowing I was part of a spiritual community stretching back in time as far as my eye could see.

This also gave me a love for old people, including their curved spines, wrinkled faces, and gnarled hands. These were the wise ones, the loving ones, and I aspired some day to become one of them. This appreciation of age puts me at odds with prevailing American values, as does the fact that I continue to believe the things about God that these elders taught me.

Most of the things I was told God had done were happy things—healings, blessings, rewards. But I now know that God sometimes does things we do not experience as happy. God was also acting in the defeat, humiliation, and affliction referred to in this psalm, and in the similar events I later experienced in my own life. Occasionally, it takes an adversity to return us to our senses. But God is there, with us, for us, regardless—as "in the days of old."

Would I recognize God in my own life today had my forebears not taught me to recognize him "in the days of old?" Possibly not. And now that I am old enough to remember my own "days of old," what am I teaching my own children?

৫৪ 44.17

All this has come upon us;
yet we have not forgotten you,
nor have we betrayed your covenant.

This psalm contains dramatic mood shifts. It begins with a retelling of the Lord's great acts of deliverance in the past. Then come groans arising out of present adversity, followed by perplexing, gnawing questions about God's apparent indifference. The psalm concludes with a plea for God to reassert himself on behalf of his people.

Taken as a whole, the psalm is a striking expression of how to deal with hardship and disappointment. There is no easy piety here—no "God must have his reasons," no "God never gives us more than we can handle," no "It will all work out in the end." Rather, the pain, the confusion, the doubt are faced head on and poured out onto the page.

The psalmist sees the people's present hardships as an act of God—"you have rejected and humbled us" (vs. 9) and are "selling your people." (vs. 12) "You thrust us down into a place of misery." (vs. 19) But even when the psalmist is convinced that the Lord has turned his back and walked away, he does not forget the Lord. Even when he is no longer sure there is anyone or anything to pray to, he continues to pray. Even when lying flat on the ground, he remains faithful to the covenant and calls out to the Lord for help.

When we are at the bottom of the pit, it is tempting to throw up our hands in hopeless resignation, and this would be an understandable, very human reaction. But these are the times, above all other times, to stay the course. The psalm-ist's final word is not of his own troubles, but of the Lord's "steadfast love."

ᏣᎳ 45.1

My heart is stirring with a noble song;
let me recite what I have fashioned for the king;
my tongue shall be the pen of a skilled writer.

In this hymn to his king (who sounds like Solomon) the psalmist combines several memorable, concrete images: the king strapping his sword to his thigh, the specific fragrances of the king's garments, the gloriously adorned princess entering the royal chamber (to say nothing of her sumptuous attendants). The psalmist was indeed a skilled writer, as he said. Nor did he entirely forget God as he rhapsodized about his king, though God is clearly not at center stage here. I find it difficult to transfer these images to Jesus, as I often do in other royal psalms. That's because the images are so—well—so worldly, so grandiose, so *macho*. Is this a hymn to be sung to the king who washed his disciples' feet? I think not.

So long as it isn't taken too seriously, there is nothing wrong with writing like this. Many a reigning monarch has encouraged and enjoyed it (take a look at the Epistle Dedicatory to the King James Bible). The psalm does, how-ever, suggest a temptation to which modern people succumb as readily as the ancients did: the temptation to look upon God as a government functionary. God does not endorse any nation, its government, or its policies. God cannot be domesticated. We rightly pray for guidance and wisdom in our rulers, but God is not a member of their staff. God does not take orders from them. God's rule transcends all nations, all governments, all policies foreign and domestic—and it is expressed not in lording it over others, but in serving them.

℘ 46.11

Be still, then, and know that I am God.

Most modern people rarely experience stillness. Televisions banish stillness from our homes. Talk shows and tapes banish it from our automobiles. Even in churches, people are uncomfortable with silence. We have grown accustomed to telephones ringing, horns honking, cash registers clanging, and voices complaining, criticizing, demanding, defending, contending. We exhaust ourselves running about, vainly striving to satisfy all the noises that fill the air around us. Our engines are always running in high gear; we have forgotten how to let them idle or turn them off. We are never still.

If we would know God, let us learn to be still. There is an outer stillness and an inner stillness. Outer stillness occurs when distracting sounds are eliminated from our surroundings. It can be achieved by driving to some remote place, turning the car engine off, and sitting there—or in many homes, simply by getting up an hour earlier.

Outer stillness encourages inner stillness but is not a prerequisite for it. Inner stillness nourishes the soul. It is the silencing of that clashing in our minds of frivolous thoughts, needless anxieties, and vain desires. It comes only if we make space for it, and it comes slowly, like the stillness after a train or airplane has passed by—the noise doesn't end in an instant, but fades away. For some, a period of several days in silence at a monastery or retreat house is helpful. For others, 20 minutes of what is called "centering prayer" brings them to silence. In time, we can discover what will create stillness in our lives, and with practice, we can learn to reside in that silence. It is there that God, who has been with us all along, can speak, make himself known, and disclose to us who he is and who we can become.

❧ 47.1

Clap your hands, all you peoples;
shout to God with a cry of joy.

I'm trying to envision how the typical Episcopal or Anglican worshiper in many parts of the world would respond if the priest read these liturgical instructions and expected them to be carried out. I've seen clapping, some of it in sophisticated rhythms, and shouting, often in response to preaching, in Anglican churches in various parts of Africa. But one rarely sees such spontaneity and enthusiasm in the Anglican and Episcopal churches of the West, and there are vast regions of the church where such behavior is not only unknown, but unimaginable.

It's a pity. Sedate, quiet worship has its place, and there are times when we want and need it. It can direct us inward where we can be still and listen for the voice of the Lord. Moreover, feelings of excitement, a kind of spiritual titillation, sometimes pass for Christian commitment. We can surely grant that excessive emotionalism in church can be a dangerous thing and at the same time acknowledge that it's a danger which, alas, hardly threatens many congregations. We are more often at risk from the opposite peril: worship that is bland, bleak, and boring; prayers recited by rote while the mind is elsewhere; hymns more mumbled than sung. Our liturgies may contain lovely words, but we read them as if we were reading the telephone book. An occasional clap or shout might do us good.

The Christian gospel is good news. That is what the word "gospel" means. It's about life out of death, release from bondage. Perhaps our problem is that it is no longer news to us because we've heard it so many times. Those who hear the Christian story for the first time often clap and shout. Maybe the rest of us should join them now and then.

❧ 47.2a

For the LORD Most High is to be feared.

Modern Christians, including Prayer Book revisers, like to replace the word "fear" with the word "reverence." This is like adding water to soup—the taste is much the same, only weaker. The word "reverence" can suggest a polite, trivial little religion, as when parents enjoin their children to show "reverence" in church (meaning they should sit still) or when someone "reverences" the altar (by giving a slight bow).

The stronger word "fear" is better, even with the connotation of evil which it sometimes carries. God is not evil. The fear with which we approach God has nothing to do with divine malevolence. It is more like our fear of an earthquake or a tornado. These are not evil powers, but they are beyond our control and manipulation. We must come to terms with them as they are; there is no compromising or bargaining.

When we try to compromise with God ("Let's redefine our terms in the light of modern understandings") or strike a bargain with God ("If you will grant me this, I promise to..."), we show that we no longer fear God. God becomes a mere pal. This is dangerous, like mistaking a hurricane for a tropical breeze.

A healthy humility is the mirror image of a healthy fear of God, and as the fear of God has vanished from many modern liturgies, so has humility. Humility is not groveling. It is an acknowledgment that we are not in charge—of anything. While we are not pawns, moved about at will by a higher force, the outcome of our plans and decisions is always beyond our control. Traditional images of God on a throne in heaven, creating and ruling the world, are not mere children's fancies which the modern world has outgrown. They point to an important truth, that "the Lord Most High is to be feared" and that we depart from his ways at our own risk.

Beautiful and lofty, the joy of all the earth,
is the hill of Zion,
the very center of the world and the city
of the great King.
God is in her citadels;
he is known to be her sure refuge.

It is fitting that those who love the Lord should reverence and adorn his temple. We construct our churches so as to suggest something of God—divine goodness, divine beauty, divine power. Especially divine power. How many cathedrals and churches do you know that resemble fortresses, with stone pillars, thick walls, and towering roof lines? A certain triumphalism soon creeps in. My God can whip your God, so don't mess with him.

That's what we see in this psalm. The loving-kindness, justice, and guidance of God are mentioned, but it is God's power, seen in the temple on Mount Zion, that is stressed. The psalmist notes the temple's beauty, but he celebrates it chiefly for its strength. The temple sits like a castle atop the holy mountain, the center of the world, providing security for the chosen ones, but terrorizing others so that they tremble, writhe, and flee when they see it.

This is an intermediate understanding of God. It is not the last word. God does not want to terrorize people with his power. That would defeat his purpose. God does not even seek to attract people with his beauty. The image of God reigning from his temple, whether in power or in beauty, is incomplete—because God displays his strength in weakness, exercises his power chiefly in showing mercy. We serve God out of gratitude because God does not demand to be served, but chooses to serve us. God does not sit in church waiting to be acknowledged, but goes out in search of his lost and beloved children. That is the heart of the Christian message. Those who picture God merely sitting on a throne waiting to be adored know something about God, but not much.

ꝏ 49.9

For we see that the wise die also;
like the dull and stupid they perish
and leave their wealth to those who come
after them.

What will your legacy be? People want to leave a permanent mark behind when they die, and they often want their name on it: a grave marker at the very least, or a published book, an endowed academic chair, a building or town bearing their name—or children to perpetuate their name. It is part of our longing for immortality.

But it won't work. Even presidents, Olympic medalists, and popes will eventually be forgotten. The great names of antiquity—Alexander the Great, Cyrus, and Julius Caesar—will someday no longer be spoken or known. One of Caesar's successors as Roman emperor, Marcus Aurelius, said it well: "Perhaps the desire of the fleeting thing called fame torments you. See how soon everything is forgotten, and look at the chaos of infinite time on each side of the present, and the emptiness of applause, and the fickleness and lack of judgment in those who pretend to give praise, and the narrowness of its domain, and be quiet at last." Or as an acquaintance of mine once said, not very sensitively, on the occasion of the death of a friend, "When the preacher said at Henry's funeral that 'Dear Henry will never be forgotten,' falser words were never spoken!"

But if for having known us, one soul finds the courage to carry on, one life is brightened, one lost sheep finds its way into the arms of God, is that not legacy enough? Or perhaps it is legacy enough to have loved and enjoyed the company of God and God's creatures for our allotted time, and given them pleasure in our company. Better, in any case, would such a legacy be than a towering monument with our name chiseled into the base.

⊂⊘ 49.10

Their graves shall be their homes for ever,
their dwelling places from generation
to generation,
though they call the lands after their
own names.

Only verse 15, with its hint of resurrection, saves this psalm from being a blatant assertion of nihilism, the denial of all belief and meaning. It reminds me of the old Peggy Lee song,

"Is that all there is?" The implied answer: "You bet that's all there is, and it ain't much." If this psalm and the Book of Ecclesiastes, which takes a similar view, were the only things in the Bible, the Bible would be a very dreary book. We must balance these passages against the rest of scripture.

But writings such as this psalm do have their place. They can help bring down to earth one who has taken to fanciful vanities. Do we imagine that our wisdom will gain us immortality? Think again. Do we trust in our great wealth? That's foolish, because we can't take it with us, or even determine what happens to it after we die. Do we name cities after ourselves? Lenin and Trujillo did that, but the names were changed back to St. Petersburg and Santo Domingo after Lenin and Trujillo died. Do we hope to immortalize ourselves through our children? They will live their own lives, not relive ours, and within a few generations, we will have been reduced to an old photograph in someone's attic, and even that will eventually be discarded. We are all like the beasts. Wise and foolish, rich and poor, famous and obscure—all shall die and return to the dirt from which we came.

In the light of this psalm, the pompous, grasping, powerful, vain, self-righteous, arrogant, condescending, and imperious all appear ludicrous. The psalm fosters humility. But I'm glad it's not the last word.

ଓଃ 50.7b

O Israel, I will bear witness against you;
for I am God, your God.

This is one of the most startling lines in the entire Bible—because it is spoken by God. The ancient Israelites had a strong sense that the Lord had chosen them of all the peoples of the earth. They had been nobodies, just a rag-tag bunch of slaves somewhere in the desert. Then, seemingly out of nowhere, the Lord appeared to Moses and initiated a covenant—"I shall be your God and you shall be my people." He then safely guided Israel through 40 years in the Sinai wilderness and settled them in the Promised Land. This tale is told again and again in the Bible, including in several psalms.

But for what exactly did the Lord choose the Israelites? A presumptuous complacency soon emerged, which regarded being chosen as an entitlement to special favors. All the responsibility was on God's side and all the benefits on Israel's side. This, too, can be found in the Bible, including some psalms. But not in this psalm. This psalmist debunks such false security. When the people of God begin to see themselves as chosen for privilege rather than for service, God will witness against them. The chosen people may be startled at the results when God acts through some other, presumably not chosen, nation—"Ah, Assyria, the rod of my anger, the staff of my fury!" (Isaiah 10:5)

The temptation to domesticate God into a kind of poster boy for patriotic causes still thrives today. Domesticated deities are especially popular in wartime. Heads of state refer to other nations and their leaders as "evil" and to their wars against them as "crusades," and the people believe what they hear. But God is not tricked by those who play such games with his name. God does not turn his back on us, but sees, and bears witness—and God's testimony determines the verdict. Will God speak for us or against us?

ℭℜ 50.10

For all the beasts of the forest are mine,
the herds in their thousands upon the hills.

John MacNaughton, retired bishop of West Texas, tells this story: A Louisiana law firm was asked to conduct a title search for a piece of property. They successfully traced the title back to the Louisiana Purchase of 1803, but their clients were not satisfied. The search went on. Finally, the law firm wrote the following letter to their clients: "Gentlemen: Be advised that in the year 1803, the United States of America acquired the territory of Louisiana from the Republic of France, by purchase. The Republic of France, in turn, acquired title from the Spanish Crown, by conquest; the Spanish Crown having obtained it by virtue of the discoveries of one Christopher Columbus, who had been authorized to undertake his voyage by Isabella, Queen of Spain, who obtained sanction for the journey from the Pope, the Vicar of Christ, who is the Son and Heir of Almighty God, who made Louisiana."

God does not need anything to which we hold title. He owns it already—what we call our ownership is a fiction.

God dreamed up everything that is, then made it, and now sustains it. He allows one human being and then another the use of it for a time. We die and someone else gets it for a while, or the stock market falls and someone else gets it before we die. God doesn't need it, anyway. What God wants from us is a relationship. He wants our hearts and minds, our time and energy, our lives. God has given himself to us in the person of Jesus Christ, and he longs for that devotion to be returned—for our own good. Don't try to buy off God with a big check. Everything already belongs to God, anyway, and besides, it isn't your money that God wants—it's you.

❧ 51.2

Wash me through and through from my wickedness and cleanse me from my sin.

This psalm, read on Ash Wednesday, is perhaps the best known expression of penitence in the Bible. Although it is traditionally attributed to King David after his adultery with Bathsheba (II Samuel 12), most scholars discount the tradition of Davidic authorship. In any case, the psalm plumbs the depths of penitence as fully as any piece of writing in the Bible.

When Christians confess their sins in church, I suspect many believe they are asking God to overlook their guilt, pretend it's not there, to whisper something like, "Oh, it's all right; I love you anyway." That's not what we have in this psalm. Look at the verbs the psalmist uses in asking God to remove his guilt: *blot*

out...wash me through and through...cleanse me...purge me.
Those are action verbs. The psalmist sees his sin as a stain, so he prays that God blot it up. Have you ever asked God to blot you? He sees it as dirt and grime, so he prays that he be washed through and through. Think of God doing his laundry and of yourself as a soiled garment. God doesn't have a washing machine—he does his laundry by hand, soaking you in sudsy water, working the suds into all your threads, then rinsing you and squeezing the dirt out of you. Or in the psalmist's most vivid image, he asks God to purge him, to make him vomit, to clean out his insides by causing him to throw up all the bile and impurities that make him sick.

None of these images refers to anything the psalmist has done. If you think of sin as bad things you have done (or good things left undone), think again. Sin is a condition, not a behavior. It's more like being sick or incapacitated than like doing something to endanger your health, more like being broken than getting broken, more like being lost than wandering off. Bad behavior has something to do with sin, but it's the result, the by-product, not the thing itself.

৯ 51.6

Indeed, I have been wicked from my birth,
a sinner from my mother's womb.

This line is often dismissed as ridiculous—how can a baby be wicked? Babies are cuddly and adorable, we tell ourselves.

But it's usually just our own babies about whom we feel that way. Other people's babies can sometimes be a nuisance. The truth is that all babies are a nuisance much of the time, even our own. Far from being dismissable, this line from the psalm makes sense in terms of human experience. People are born selfish. The best evidence of it is the behavior of infants—they scream to demand that their every want be satisfied immediately, with no thought of what other people might need or want. It's a good thing infants are so cute, because otherwise, no one would put up with them for one minute. Concern for something greater than one's own comfort must be taught, and fortunately, most infants prove reformable as they mature.

This line makes sense theologically as well. The doctrine of "original sin" is sometimes pooh-poohed today. That's unfortunate. It points to a profound truth, the fact that merely to be human, even from the moment of conception, is to be caught, trapped in a set of broken relationships from which we are powerless to escape. St. Augustine went too far in locating "original sin" in the act of procreation—sexuality is not the problem, nor is it more innately sinful than anything else in human experience. Our sexuality is broken, but no more so than everything else about us. Apart from that small point, however, Augustine was right on target. Sin is indeed universal in human experience and unavoidable. No sooner are we conceived than we become part of a broken universe, where selfishness, injustice, competition, and betrayal run rampant.

Think of that the next time you wonder why the church baptizes infants.

❧ 51.11

Create in me a clean heart, O God,
and renew a right spirit within me.

Full as this psalm is of expressions of penitence, there is just one brief reference to anything the psalmist will do to make amends or express his regret—he will teach the ways of the Lord to the wicked (vs 14). Apart from that, the psalm is entirely about what God will do. It isn't the psalmist who, through the force of his character and willpower, makes a new start, leads a new life, reforms himself—God does that. The psalmist does not say, "I'll clean my heart up, O God, and renew a right spirit within myself." He doesn't say it because he knows he couldn't do it if he did say it. Sin is an addiction, and as every recovering addict knows, you don't heal yourself. God heals you or you die in your sickness.

We can, of course, swear off certain behaviors, and sometimes we actually succeed when we swear off something—heavy drinkers do get sober; angry people do learn to control their tempers. But a sober alcoholic is still a sinner, and a temper held in check doesn't address the rage within. It isn't enough to say, "I'm sorry and I'll try to do better," even if you really are sorry and even if you succeed in doing better. It takes an act of God to set things right, and that's what the psalmist prays for. This entire psalm is about the power of God to heal and change people. God does this not by simply waving a wand or reciting a magic incantation. Rather, God goes to work, gets his hands dirty, rescues people. True penitence isn't regret for the past; it is a changed present and future, and only God can effect the change.

Our part is simply to agree to let God work in us, to invite God into our lives. That's what this psalmist is doing.

◌ 51.18b

A broken and contrite heart, O God,
you will not despise.

Heartbreak can come from many directions. Betrayal by a friend, infidelity in marriage, children who turn their backs on us, hopes dashed, justice denied, innocence betrayed, sickness, grief—no human life is spared heartbreak. When heartbreak comes to us, we can respond in several ways: We can grow angry and bitter. We can lash out at those we think have wronged us. We can sink into cynicism and despair. We can deaden our feelings and sedate ourselves with alcohol, drugs, sex, or work. Or we can listen for the voice of our God who will not despise the broken heart.

It is not necessary to pray for a broken heart—sooner or later, our hearts will be broken without our asking. Neither is it necessary to desire a broken heart—only the spiritually sick *want* to be miserable. But if we look for God in the midst of our heartbreak, we discover that God does not despise the broken heart and we may even come to thank him for it.

Oswald Chambers has said, "If through a broken heart God can bring His purposes to pass in the world, then thank Him for breaking your heart." And what are God's purposes in the world? God seeks to heal and restore our souls by uniting us to himself, and through him to one another, in our brokenness. God desires nothing more than that we turn to him, allow him to enfold us in his arms, dry our tears, and whisper into our ears that he loves us. Moreover, when resting in the arms of God, we discover that we are not alone, but that others rest there alongside us. When we turn to God and allow God to do this, we find the peace of God that passes understanding and we discover the secret of contentment.

ଔ 52.4

You love all words that hurt,
O you deceitful tongue.

There's not much doubt what the psalmist most dislikes about his enemy—it's the sound of the man's voice. He refers to his enemy's boasting, his lies, his hurtful words, and likens his enemy's tongue to "a sharpened razor." There are people like that, both men and women, and I feel about them just as the psalmist does—if they would just *zip it up!*

But what if I am not the one speaking the psalm, but the one of whom it is spoken, not the one wishing someone else would hold off from sharp words, but the one hurling the sharp words? Could someone be thinking these thoughts *about me?* I know they could. In fact, I know they have thought this of me, and with good reason. I love words. I cultivate them. I know how to use them and I know how to misuse them. I have used my tongue to get a laugh at another's expense. I have used it to manipulate others into doing what I wanted. I have used it to demean others when I did not share their feelings. I have used it to intimidate the weak and mock the ignorant. I believe and hope I have not often spoken in these ways, and I have repented of it when I have been made aware of it afterwards—but I cannot pretend that every word that has passed my lips has been worthy of one claiming to follow Jesus.

But because God forgives the sinner who comes to him, I can see myself simultaneously as the one of whom this psalm is spoken and as the one speaking it. Unworthy though my words have sometimes been, yet God loves me and I can say that I am "like a green olive tree in the house of God; I trust in the mercy of God for ever and ever." (vs. 8)

❧ 53.1a

The fool has said in his heart, "There is no God."

I've said there is no God. Sometimes I've said it intellectually. Looking at the disorder and evil in the world, I concluded there could not be a God (or if there were, I wanted nothing to do with him). Sometimes I've said it arrogantly. Full of myself and ready to conquer everything in sight, I felt no need for God. Sometimes I've said it mournfully. Crushed and ground down, I cried out to God, and when I heard no answer, I concluded no one was there.

Was I a fool to say there was no God? I suppose I was, but the world is home to vast numbers of such fools, and I suspect most people have played the part of that fool now and again. At no time, however, was God entirely out of my view. When my intellect ceased to believe, I still wanted to believe and I still tried to believe. When I felt no need for God, I still wanted to please the God whom I did not need. When I heard no answer to my cries, I cried out all the more to the God I suspected was not there, for I desired solace from no one else. Even when I did not believe in God, I could not forget God. God was always there, on the edge of my vision, just out of sight, around the corner, agitating, unrecognized but beckoning. It seemed that although I might have left God, God had not left me.

Looking back now, I see that my attitudes and behaviors mattered only in that they affected me—they left me vulnerable and bereft—but they did not affect the fact of God. Human foolishness does not carry the day. We may say, think, and do what we will. In the end, God will be God.

‰ 53.3

Every one has proved faithless;
all alike have turned bad;
  there is none who does good; no, not one.

Most of this psalm is a repeat of Psalm 14. This verse, which appears in both psalms, should restrain even the most rosy-eyed optimist. Everyone is rotten. No exceptions. St. Paul concluded the same thing: "For there is no distinction, since all have sinned and fall short of the glory of God." (Rom. 3:23). But Paul was not discouraged. He continued: "They are justified by his grace as a gift, through the redemption which is in Christ Jesus."

The church gives a cursory bow in the direction of Paul and his concluding thought, but sometimes that's all we give him. Several scandals have wracked my denomination in recent years. There was a case of embezzlement by a national church official a few years back. Some bishops have betrayed the confidence their dioceses placed in them. And there have been a few seamy sexual episodes. "Our leaders have betrayed us—off with their heads!" some have shouted. Of course our leaders have betrayed us. And we have betrayed them. We have all betrayed each other, and we continue to do it. When we look at the person in the next pew, we see a betrayer, a disreputable sham, and when he looks at us, he sees the same thing. There is no distinction. Every one has proved faithless.

Our job is to pray for our brothers and sisters, not to castigate them. God puts up with them, even loves them, apparently, just as God loves us. I assume some are greater sinners than others, but we can't know about that, so we must leave the sorting out of sinners to God. It is enough for us to know that we are among them and that God forgives and embraces us all.

I will offer you a freewill sacrifice
and praise your Name, O Lᴏʀᴅ, for it is good.
For you have rescued me from every trouble,
and my eye has seen the ruin of my foes.

Shall we give God a little gift and praise him because we have
the pleasure of watching our enemies fall to their ruin? That
does sound like fun! Watching our enemies in defeat can be
even more fun than being rescued ourselves. They were so
arrogant, so intransigent, so insistent. Just look at them now,
lying there in disgrace!

Be careful of such thoughts. When we are under attack,
it is natural to pray, as this psalmist does, that God will save
us from our enemies. This is a worthy prayer, acknowledging
that all power is ultimately in God's hands. It is a short step
from this prayer, however, to another prayer, that our enemies
be humiliated and destroyed. It may also be natural to pray
this second prayer, but it is not a worthy prayer, for it focuses
not on God's power to save, but on our desire for revenge.

There is a second reason as well to be careful of such
thoughts, namely, that we are not the only ones who can
entertain them. Even as we pray for the humiliation of our
enemy, someone—perhaps the very enemy against whom we
are praying—may be praying for our humiliation. Wouldn't it
be better—and more in the spirit of Jesus—if we all prayed
for reconciliation, forgiveness, and a change of heart?

And there's that enemy within. What of him? What of
the spiritual cancers that rot our souls? Many of us cling to
those enemies, feed them, applaud them. If it is our enemies

within who are to be ruined, might that not hurt just a bit? Are we really prepared to request that our deepest desires be humiliated and then praise God for it after it's done?

℘ 55.7

And I said, "Oh, that I had wings like a dove!
I would fly away and be at rest.

Betrayed by his friends, the psalmist explores the rich variety of his feelings. Among his feelings is the fantasy of being able to fly away from it all and leave everything behind. It's a fantasy known to many who have felt trapped. I have known husbands and wives trapped in a bad marriage, children trapped in homes with negligent or abusive parents, penitentiary inmates trapped behind barbed wire fences, workers trapped in dead-end jobs, invalids trapped in bodies that no longer work, entire neighborhoods trapped in poverty, entire nations trapped by corrupt or tyrannical heads of state. All of them fantasized about flying away.

Sometimes we are not really trapped and a means of flying away can be found, but often this is not the case. Indulging the fantasy of flying away is not a bad thing; it may even be good for the soul. When outward circumstances entrap us, the mind can still fly free. I recall one woman confined to a wheelchair in a convalescent home. When I met her, she identified herself in a way that startled me at first. "My name is Bessie, and I'm a tennis player," she said. I thought to myself, "Well if you're a tennis player, then I'm the patriarch of Constantinople." But then

I had a second thought: This woman once enjoyed playing tennis, and in her mind, she still enjoyed it. She still ran across the court and returned the difficult backhand. She did not let herself be defined by the body I saw sitting in that wheelchair. She was a blessed, wise, and triumphant soul. Should I ever find myself in similar circumstances, may the spirit I witnessed in her be the spirit that lives in me!

❧ 56.8

You have noted my lamentation;
put my tears into your bottle;
are they not recorded in your book?

What an odd image. Why would the psalmist ask God to bottle his tears? I don't know. Bottling something is a way of preserving it, so presumably the psalmist wanted God to preserve his tears. I can think of three possible reasons why:

First (and most likely, I think), the psalmist may simply have wanted God to remember his grief. The prayer is akin to a plea common in the Psalms, "Do not forsake me, O Lord." If God preserved the psalmist's tears, God could never entirely forget the psalmist and his grief. They would have a lasting place with God (even if on a back shelf in some remote closet). The desire of the suffering not to be forgotten is a natural one.

Second, the psalmist may have wanted God to preserve his tears so that the psalmist could enjoy pulling out the bottle and gazing at them now and then.

Some people relish and nurture their martyrdom; they feel the role becomes them—"Poor, innocent, suffering me! Just look at my tears. Here they are, conveniently displayed in this clear glass cruet—see them? But I shall carry on!"

Third (an unlikely but intriguing possibility), the psalmist might have wanted God to bottle his tears so that he could pour them out when he was ready. I was once feeling sorry for myself and a friend suggested I place all my grief in a bottle, symbolically, then pour it out on the ground. I did, and the act of pouring my tears into the ground helped dispel the grief.

℘ 57.7

My heart is firmly fixed, O God,
my heart is fixed;
I will sing and make melody.

"Grant that among the sundry and manifold changes of the world, our hearts may surely there be fixed where true joys are to be found." So prayed Archbishop Cranmer in one of his most famous collects.

Some hearts don't seem fixed anywhere. Restless souls drift from one thing to another, trying first this and then that, never making a firm commitment to anything or anyone. I once knew a woman who was fondly referred to as a "church hopper." She worshiped in a congregation for a year or so, then was suddenly gone and later found to be worshiping in another congregation. This behavior she repeated many times. Some people move from job to job, or more tragically, from relationship to relationship or from marriage to marriage.

Others' hearts are fixed. They persevere through lean years and fat years, never taking their eye off the prize. But these, too, can fail to find what they seek if their hearts are fixed on something that cannot deliver true joys. Fame, power, wealth, and beauty promise joy but do not deliver it, and those who devote their lives to chasing such things are sad souls in the end. This psalmist's heart was firmly fixed on the greatness and kindness of God. He says he "will sing and make melody." The reason was that his heart was fixed where true joys are to be found.

ଊ 57.8

Wake up, my spirit;
awake, lute and harp;
   I myself will waken the dawn.

There is nothing inherently special about one time of day over another. Some people are at their best in the morning, others at night, others when the mood hits them. For this psalmist, apparently, as for me, morning is the favored time. I usually awaken without an alarm, sometimes when all is still dark and quiet. This verse often comes to mind as I imagine myself waking the dawn, summoning the new day, beckoning the sun to show its face among the trees.

Waiting and watching for the first hint of dawn is holy time for me. My senses seem particularly keen at that hour. Sounds of songbirds, the wind, the creaking of the house, and distant traffic are clear and sharp. When I sit out of doors before dawn, my lungs feel the cool night air filling them. I feel the night breezes, the softness of the shirt against my skin, the firmness of the chair beneath me. I see the stars or moonlight through the clouds, the streetlight at the corner, the bare outline of the house. Or on a cloudy night in a remote spot, there is nothing to see but the darkness, which makes sounds and smells and touches all the more acute.

It is good to identify your holy time, then block it out and save it for holy uses. Do not let the cares of the day intrude except to surrender them to God. Spend the time doing nothing, just resting in the Lord. Let your senses remind you of God's goodness in your life.

ೞ 58.1-2

Do you indeed decree righteousness, you rulers?
    do you judge the peoples with equity?
No; you devise evil in your hearts,
    and your hands deal out violence in the land.

As I write these words, I have been teaching for several months in what Transparency International has named the second most corrupt country in the world. Police routinely hold up motorists for cash. State governors let out contracts for road construction but the work is never done and the funds never accounted for. Public school teachers in the state where I teach have not been paid in seven months, although the government collected funds to pay them. The state governor here made a big show recently of donating $10,000 to help construct a new cathedral, but the bishop turned the money down and told him to pay his teachers with it. The governor took back the money but the teachers remain unpaid. How had the governor come by such money, anyway, a vast sum by local standards? He didn't explain that.

This psalm is written about such governors. The psalmist vents his anger in vivid images—"break their teeth, pull their fangs." The citizens of the country where I now teach, however, are surprisingly accepting of the corruption from which they suffer. They pray about it and trust in the Lord. Considered as a way of getting by day to day, there is wisdom in their approach—why get angry over what you cannot change?

But that's not the only way to think about it. "Well, yes," I say to myself (and occasionally to them), "but if you never grow angry over injustice, things might never get better. You pray that God will do something about the evil that surrounds you. Perhaps God does intend to do something—and perhaps he wants to do it *through you*."

℘ 59.9

But you, O LORD, you laugh at them;
you laugh all the ungodly to scorn.

The first thing God is seen to do in the Psalter is to laugh (2:4). But the laughter of God isn't a major biblical motif. The Bible contains only three references to God's laughter. All three are in the Psalms (the other is at 37:14) and all three are unsettling. The Hebrew *sachaq*, like the English "laugh," can carry either a light-hearted meaning or a derisive, mocking meaning. Clearly, in these three references, it carries the latter meaning. There is nothing light-hearted about any of these verses—all three are about mocking laughter. Sinners mock or laugh at God, but God has the last, mocking laugh when he overtrumps the laughter of the wicked.

But are we to think that God actually takes delight in the demise of the wicked, or is the psalmist projecting his own feelings onto God? If God loves sinners and desires that they turn from their wickedness and live (as we've been told he does), I can imagine God's grieving over their destruction, but how could he enjoy it?

And what of that other kind of laughter, the light-hearted kind? The Bible contains no explicit references to God's laughing merrily (although the Genesis account of the birth of Isaac hints at it), but an argument from silence is a weak argument. Could God have a sense of humor? Is the notion of a giggling God entirely out of bounds? Happy laughter is not incompatible with a passion for justice and truth. Among earthly creatures, only human beings have a sense of humor. Some animals laugh when they are tickled, but humor is human, and uniquely so. Only humans laugh at a joke or gag. Genesis says God created humans in his own image—could the ability to laugh be part of what we have in common with God?

ca 60.8

Moab is my wash-basin,
on Edom I throw down my sandal to claim it,
and over Philistia will I shout in triumph.

Here is an expression of ethnic scorn second to none. The three peoples mentioned here are all traditional enemies of Israel, and the psalmist envisions God pouring dirty water onto one of them, beating another with his shoe, and shouting down the third. Clearly, God had not yet done these things at the time of writing, for the psalmist bemoans the fact that it appears God is angry at Israel and has cast her off—"you no longer go out, O God, with our armies." (vs. 10)

This verse illustrates a tension within the Hebrew Bible. Some biblical authors, particularly the earlier ones, see the Lord's choice of Israel as a guarantee of favor and protection in military campaigns against other "not chosen" peoples. This psalmist is of that view and is at pains to remind God of God's obligation to his chosen people. Other biblical authors, however, see the Lord's choice of Israel as a call to service, even to shine as a beacon of righteousness in the world (Isa. 42). By this view, Israel is the one with something to do, and if Israel refuses to answer her call implied in being the chosen people, the Lord will chasten her until she turns and amends her ways.

Which is the right understanding of chosenness? As the new Israel, the Christian church has usually understood it in the second sense (but by no means always, as Jews and Muslims through the centuries can attest). And what of the old Israel? The question is a burning one even today, for

Moab, Edom, and Philistia were the ancestors of the modern Palestinians. Is the modern nation of Israel called to be a light to her neighbors, and if so, how is that done? And what of America? Many Americans see their nation as God's agent in the world. Are our behaviors and policies motivated by a call to serve as a light to others?

ca 61.1

Hear my cry, O God,
*   and listen to my prayer.*

This short verse could stand as a summary of more than a third of the biblical psalms. The things prayed for vary, but pleading with God to listen to the psalmists' requests is a recurring theme. For many modern people as well, prayer consists largely, perhaps even entirely, of asking God for things.

God wants us to bring our requests to him, but petition is only one part of a full prayer life. A preoccupation with asking for things easily becomes self-centeredness. Praise, adoration, and thanksgiving for blessings already received draw the spirit away from self and to God. Moreover, when our prayers do focus on ourselves (as sometimes they should), it is important to include penitence and surrender of the will alongside our requests.

God loves us more than we love ourselves and knows better than we what is best for us. The best petition, therefore, does not tell God what to do. I do not hesitate to ask God for specific things, especially when I am deeply troubled, because God already knows what is in my heart, so there would be no use in pretending otherwise. But I have learned, even at such times, to end my plea with something like this: "I have told you what I want, Lord, though you knew it anyway. I hope you will grant my request. But most of all, give me what you desire for me; give what I need, even if it is not what I have asked. It is you that I need and want, Lord, more than anything in this world. I leave this concern, as I leave all things, in your hands."

○ℜ 62.6

For God alone my soul in silence waits;
truly, my hope is in him.

We spend much of our lives waiting anxiously. We wait for our children to grow older so we won't feel tied down. We wait for a better job. We wait for good health. We wait until we can retire and live a more leisurely life. We wait for someone to die and leave us a bequest. We wait for a chance to get even with someone. When we let our happiness depend on some future event, often something unlikely to happen and perhaps something that wouldn't be best for us anyway, our waiting becomes tense and anxious.

The key to waiting contentedly is to focus upon God. It is important to remember three things:

First, God is present, even as we wait. Often we do not perceive God in the present moment, but that does not mean he is absent from us. The awareness of God comes and goes—that's what we actually wait for—but God never departs from us.

Second, God can solve our problems for us, and often does. But our real problem is usually not what we think it is—too little money, not enough friends, a handicap of some sort—but our unreadiness to receive God into our lives.

Third, we don't need something God can give us, something external to God, but God himself. God not only gives us our salvation; he *is* our salvation.

℘ 63.1

O God, you are my God: eagerly I seek you;
my soul thirsts for you, my flesh faints for you,
as in a barren and dry land where there
is no water.

Thirst, faintness, barrenness—these are the words with which the psalmist describes his sense of the absence of God. When God seems to withdraw, it is as if a once green valley is now arid and parched. The soul that formerly flourished is left languishing, feeling empty and bereft. But the memory of happier and more fruitful times remains, producing a longing for the return of the confidence and serenity of bygone days.

For some, these barren times come often, for others only occasionally. They come frequently to me. The barrenness is usually brief in duration, although twice in my life it lasted several years. Those of us who experience such times must not let them define us. The temptation is to wallow in our doubt and confusion, but that need not happen. It is a choice. The other and better choice is to remember earlier times when we sensed the presence of God, to thank God for them, and to await their return. The sense of the presence of God is like the tide—it goes out, but it also comes in.

Barren times can also be occasions of unusual spiritual growth, for they remind us how much we love God. It is as in a marriage—prolonged separation from my wife does more than anything else to bring home to me how much I love her, whereas an uninterrupted cozy intimacy, with God or spouse, can lead to taking our loved one for granted.

❧ 64.7

The human mind and heart are a mystery;
but God will loose an arrow at them,
and suddenly they will be wounded.

The context of this verse suggests that the psalmist believes it's the wicked whose hearts God will wound, but when he wrote the psalm, it was the psalmist's own heart that was wounded—by the successes of the wicked and God's apparent willingness to let them succeed. Could it be that not only the wounds of the wicked, but also the psalmist's own wounds were the result of an "arrow" from God? Could God even have allowed the wicked to prosper in order to wound the psalmist's heart, to challenge the psalmist in some way?

The psalmist acknowledges that the human mind and heart are a mystery, beyond his understanding. That includes the psalmist's own mind and heart. God also is a mystery. Someone once defined a mystery as something "infinitely knowable," that is, something about which there is always more to discover and know. The psalmist, like many of us, knows very little about what really matters.

Does God wound those whom he loves? We don't know. We can only guess, based on limited human experience. Perhaps our experience of parenthood is our best clue. A responsible parent protects, disciplines, and trains her child, respecting the child's dignity and never wounding a child violently, maliciously, or to gain power or control. But the child may not know or understand this and may feel "wounded" on occasion. Like a child, we know not what we need, nor how God will provide it. Sometimes we must simply trust that God knows more about us than we know about ourselves, continually loves us, and acts for us and not against us, even when we are wounded.

℘ 65.2

To you that hear prayer shall all flesh come,
because of their transgressions.

All flesh shall come to the one who hears prayer—*all* flesh. Awareness that God loves everyone emerged late in the history of Israel and finds its fullest expression in the New Testament. The tendency today, as in ancient times, is to limit the circle of acceptability to those like ourselves—in belief or behavior, in race or nationality, in religious affiliation. Human beings, it seems, are forever trying to shrink the circle, while God is forever trying to expand it.

A number of years ago, I wrote a column in the local newspaper which aroused the opposition of the pastors of another Christian denomination in the community. They took me to task by name on their Sunday morning radio broadcast, assuring their listeners that since I had disseminated false teaching in the name of Christ, I would be spending eternity in a hot and desolate place. A parishioner of mine heard the broadcast and told me of it. (I never asked why she was at home listening to the radio on Sunday morning.)

Later that week, I telephoned one of the pastors of the other denomination and asked to meet with him and his colleagues. We met a few days later and talked together for over two hours. They were gracious to me, but I don't think anyone changed his mind about anything. I hope, though, that I at least established that, while my theology could be questioned, I intended well. At the end of the meeting, I said, "One difference between us is that I believe God's arms embrace all, whereas you believe they embrace only those who agree with you. I think you and I are both going to heaven when we die, and when we get there, I won't be surprised to see you—and I hope your surprise will be a happy one when you look up and see me!"

ॐ 65.12

You crown the year with your goodness,
and your paths overflow with plenty.

Unusual in the Bible, this psalm celebrates God's power but makes no reference to historical events. History is the usual stage on which biblical authors perceive God's power displayed. Historical events are unique, unrepeatable acts—that is to say, while people are born, live, and die, and while kingdoms rise and fall time and again, this *particular* person or kingdom will not be seen again. It is in particular people and events that the Bible usually sees God's hand at work in the world, working out his purposes and designs.

This psalm, however, begins by envisioning acts of worship, centered in the Jerusalem temple, and concludes with references to agriculture. It also refers to ocean waves and to dawn and dusk. While particular worship services, particular harvests, and particular sunsets may be unrepeatable events, worship, agriculture, and the movement of heavenly bodies are recurring, cyclical phenomena. There are cycles even within history—people are born, grow up, work, fall in love, marry, and have children, and those children then do the same; dynasties and empires rise and fall. These cyclical events suggest structure, rhythm, and pattern.

This also tells us something of God. It points to the fact that even within unrepeatable history, God is not capricious or arbitrary, but consistent and reliable. The God who revealed himself in yesterday's events is the same God who acts in today's and tomorrow's events. We can count on God to be God. God's goodness and power are the same yesterday, today, and forever.

☙ 66.14

Come and listen, all you who fear God,
*   and I will tell you what he has done for me.*

Most Christians like to share their testimonies. Some may be reluctant to speak before a crowd, but in the right setting, they are eager to speak of what God has done in their lives. Christians have stories to tell of the power and love of God, and these stories are invariably personal. They are about healings, challenges, and reconciled relationships. They are about fresh starts after disappointment, failure, or betrayal. They are about being born again.

There are times to tell our stories and times not to tell our stories. Some Christians are too quick to speak, providing answers to questions that have not been asked, to people who do not wish or need to hear. I had a friend once who liked to say to me, "The Lord has laid it on my heart to tell you..." Then would follow my friend's opinion about what I should do or not do, based on something my friend had experienced. I wanted to say to my friend (but didn't), "The Lord has laid it on *my* heart to live my own life, not your life!" The trouble was that my friend didn't take the time to find out what was going on with me before laying his opinions on me. He cared more about making his point than he cared about me.

God cares about people, not about making points. If we are to speak God's word when we tell our stories, we must listen before saying anything. God is already at work in the life of the person with whom we want to share our story, and we must take the time to understand the other person before we can have any idea what God would have us say.

ᶜᴿ 67.3

Let the peoples praise you, O God;
let all the peoples praise you.

This psalm envisions a world where God is known and praised by everyone on earth. This happy vision often seems a distant and unlikely hope. But it may be closer to the truth than we realize.

Often we assume that others, especially those who differ from us in some way that reflects unfavorably on them, are not praising God. We are often mistaken about this. I visit and conduct worship services in a nearby state prison. Prior to beginning these visits, if I thought about prison inmates at all, I would have regarded them as people who needed to learn something about praising and obeying God, something I perhaps could teach them. While my friends in the penitentiary may have learned something from me, I know that I have learned more from them. They display a humility, a depth of penitence, and a fullness of grace, in grim and dehumanizing conditions, that I do not always find outside the prison walls and which often exceeds my own. I am humbled when I visit my incarcerated friends, and I praise God more honestly for knowing them. I have also heard God praised by hospital patients in great pain and by Africans in the bush with what appeared to me little for which to be thankful. These are people I would have thought lacked the time, the will, or the ability to praise God. I was wrong.

I believe we will know the reality of this psalm when we become willing to sit at the feet of those we once thought to teach.

❧ 68.3

Let the righteous be glad and rejoice before God;
let them also be merry and joyful.

Why are some so glum who claim to be close to God? Dreary
piety can strangle the soul.

I was once rector of a parish in a town where the econ-
omy was foundering and people were selling their homes and
moving out. If we had the same number of worshipers in
church this week that we had a year ago, we counted it a
major victory. The question in the back of many minds was:
Can we keep the church doors open another year? I recall
asking one crusty old man why he kept plugging away to raise
money for the church. I'm not sure what answer I expected,
but I was surprised by the answer I got: "I want this church
to last until I die so that I can be buried from it."

I remember thinking to myself that there was some-
thing missing in that answer. What was missing was joy.
When things seem to be disintegrating, in our own lives,
in the lives of those we love, or in the community around
us, we are tempted to sink into despair. "The Slough of
Despond", as Bunyan calls it, is very alluring. Is there really a
God? If so, is he really strong? Is he really good? Isn't Good
Friday in fact the definitive day of the year?

I ask such questions myself. One can't expect always
to be happy. But glum pessimism does not define the
Christian. Even when things are disintegrating, let the
righteous be glad, for above any and every circumstance,
God reigns. Some of us need to be reminded of that.

❧ 68.6

God gives the solitary a home and brings forth
prisoners into freedom;
but the rebels shall live in dry places.

There is an outward freedom and an inner freedom. Outward freedom is the absence of constraint, the ability to go and do as we please. It depends on circumstances which may be beyond our control—where we live and whether we possess the health and the means to do as we please. Inner freedom is something else. It is a condition of the soul. It is easier to achieve inner freedom if we have outward freedom, but outward freedom does not guarantee inner freedom. The opposite of inner freedom is addiction. We can become addicted to many things—alcohol or some other substance, power, sex, the acquisition of money, the internet, a relationship, even church. An addiction is anything that so dominates our thoughts and our lives that we are not in control of it—it controls us. An addict may be free of outward constraint, but his soul is trapped.

I have known wealthy and physically healthy people who were not free. Their prison was within themselves, but it was just as debilitating to the spirit as an actual prison cell, perhaps more so. I have also known prison inmates and people whose paralyzed bodies severely limited what they could do, but who were free. The difference lay within them.

Those who clutch their addictions and will not surrender them to God may be outwardly free, but are inwardly captive to passions that grip and suffocate their souls. Inner freedom is ours for the asking, but we must surrender to God first. God gives the solitary a home and brings prisoners to freedom, but only when they turn to him and make that act of surrender.

ೞ **68.9**

You sent a gracious rain, O God,
upon your inheritance;
you refreshed the land when it was weary.

Once in a while, I awaken in the early morning hours with my stomach in knots, unable to go back to sleep. When this happens, I sometimes get up and use the quiet time for prayer and meditation. Not only do I enjoy these moments, but they often help me eventually to fall asleep again.

I remember awakening one morning at 3:30, tense and preoccupied because of an incident of the previous day. I got up, went into the next room, and opened the windows. A light rain was falling outside. I heard the gentle tapping of the raindrops against the leaves of the magnolia trees and envisioned the ground gently soaking up the water that fell from the leaves. For a long time I just listened. Then I turned to the Psalms and began to read, as I do every morning (though usually at 6:30 rather than at 3:30). I like to read the Psalms straight through, in sequence, and it happened that Psalm 68 was the next one. My eye fell on this verse. In my imagination, my parched, weary soul became the ground outside my window, loosened and soothed by the falling rain. In the prayers that followed, I let go of the concerns which had troubled me and entrusted them to God.

Why, I wondered, do I spend so many waking hours tense about the events that swirl around me? Perhaps it is because I too rarely take the time to sit quietly and listen to the rain.

❧ 68.28

Send forth your strength, O God;
establish, O God, what you have
wrought for us.

What has God wrought for us?

When I was a boy, I built a tree house. I gathered spare boards and pieces of plywood and nailed them into the branches of a maple tree in our backyard. The construction was so shoddy that merely to climb into my tree house was to risk falling to the ground. An older boy named Tommy who lived nearby asked if he might share my tree house. I agreed. My tree house became *our* tree house. Tommy knew about building things. He shored up my construction, adding support beams and transforming my haphazardly assembled structure into a house fit to spend a night in. But I had to consent to let Tommy improve my work, and I had to sit quietly while he did so, learning from him as I watched.

God has transformed our lives—but until we give our consent, the transformation is only in the mind of God. Sometimes we don't even know how to give our consent. God knows what we have in us to become because he creates us and knows his work, and he must show us how to open ourselves to his working within us. But God honors our freedom and allows us to dance to whatever piper we choose. This is true both for individuals and for institutions such as congregations, dioceses, and denominations. We can bow to the altar of self-will, or we can bow to the altar of the Lord of the universe. God has wrought for us a glory like his own, but that glory remains mere potential until we say yes.

❧ 69.7

Let not those who hope in you be put to shame
through me, Lord GOD of hosts;
let not those who seek you be disgraced
because of me, O God of Israel.

St. Paul spoke of a knowledge that brings conceit (I Cor. 8:1). This is a sophisticated knowledge possessed only by a few. Paul's example had to do with meat sacrificed to idols. He knew, as did the sophisticated Corinthian Christians, that since idols have no real power, to eat such meat was a harmless act. Many, however, believed that to eat such meat was sinful, and Paul therefore advised the Corinthian Christians to refrain from eating meat sacrificed to idols so as not to offend others.

A similar situation confronts the church today. Some Christians in the sophisticated West regard homosexuality, in itself, as a morally neutral thing. The moral issue, they feel, is whether the partners are committed and monogamous and whether their union is spiritually ennobling. I suspect they may be right, but most Christians in Africa find any such relationship morally repugnant. When Western clergy bless same-sex unions, African Christians experience this as a slap in the face. Courtesy should restrain us in the West from any action that scandalizes others who hope in the Lord. Moreover, the sophisticated position is not always the godly one.

It can cut the other way, too. Gay and lesbian Christians experience the refusal to bless same-sex unions as a slap in the face. Conservative Christians in Africa and elsewhere might choose to refrain from making demands that "put to shame" fellow-believers elsewhere.

Humility should lead all of us to acknowledge at least the possibility that we could be wrong, or that the truth could extend beyond our line of vision. Caution and restraint are called for on the part of all. To demean or shame others because they see things differently than we do, especially if they reside in a culture different from our own, is arrogant and contrary to the spirit of Christ.

℞ 69.25

Let their eyes be darkened, that they may not see,
and give them continuous trembling
in their loins.

Many of the psalmists ask God to vindicate them against their enemies, but this is one of a very few psalms where vindictiveness is a dominant theme. This psalmist visualizes his enemies' suffering with graphic imagination—*"continuous trembling in their loins?"*—and he makes no effort to conceal his vengeful fantasies.

How did such hatred find its way into the scriptures? For what purpose is it there? Years ago, a friend betrayed me, causing me much trouble and heartache. For weeks I fantasized about the revenge I wanted to take against her. I rehearsed caustic speeches in my mind as I drove about town. Getting back at her began to consume my thoughts. Then one day I chanced to read this psalm. I found its sentiments offensive and I didn't like its author—and I realized that I could have written the psalm myself. As with the psalmist, a sour, vindictive self-pity had come to possess my soul. Was it possible that others found me as offensive as I found this psalmist? I realized at that moment that my problem wasn't the woman, but the vile spirit within me.

Perhaps the value of this psalm is that it invites us to take a look in the mirror. Can we see ourselves in the psalmist? The enemies posing the greatest danger to us may not be external, but internal. Resentment, brooding over slights, lust for revenge—these are like cancers of the soul which eat away at the soul's health and sap its strength. When they sprout up within us, they must be uprooted.

০৪ 70.1,5b,6b

Be pleased, O God, to deliver me;
O LORD, make haste to help me....
come to me speedily, O God....
O LORD, do not tarry.

Three times this psalmist begs God to waste no time in coming to his aid. Adversaries are mocking him and enjoying his misfortunes, and he is fed up with it. "Help me, Lord—and hurry up about it!" Such impatience can result from various circumstances, and when we're the ones in distress, the psalmist's sense of urgency is easy to understand.

When we are content with our lives, however, we find it easy to say to someone else who wants divine intervention immediately, "Now, now! you should learn to be patient and wait on the Lord!" This is not helpful to a person in distress, nor is it helpful to minimize the other's misfortunes with glib remarks such as, "Try to look for a silver lining. Just trust Jesus and everything will be all right. Take it to the Lord in prayer. It couldn't be as bad as all that. Don't you think you're overdramatizing?" Worst of all is "I understand what you're going through." Most people who say that don't understand at all and shouldn't pretend they do.

There may be wisdom in some of those responses. They are likely to fall on deaf ears, however, for a suffering man will hear them (probably correctly) as easy platitudes. A better and more supportive response would be to listen attentively and say little. The sufferer will learn whatever lessons God wishes him to learn when he is able to learn them—and that is probably not at the time he is telling God, in every other breath, to hurry up.

❧ 71.18

And now that I am old and gray-headed, O God,
do not forsake me,
till I make known your strength to this
generation
and your power to all who are to come.

I am old and gray-headed as I write these words, and I hope I
might still have some opportunity to make known the power
of God to those who shall come after me. I'll give it a try, but
I've got some doubts about it:

First, I didn't learn of the power of God myself until
I was good and ready to learn it, and that, sorry to say, was
some years after I'd received my theological degree. You can
only learn some things the hard way, and for me, the power
of God was one of those things.

Second, young people don't much listen to those who
are old and gray-headed, at least not these days and not in
America. I love being old (probably because I'm still healthy
and have things to do), but I don't kid myself about being
looked to for sage advice. Some other time and some other
place, maybe, but not now and not here.

Third, I've botched up as many things in my life as I've
done right, and I still botch things up. Moreover, there are
many important things that I know nothing about and hardly
any on which I consider myself an expert. I may be old and
gray-headed, but I'm still learning. That, in fact, is the most
delightful thing about being old and gray-headed—having
the time for new experiences and new learnings. As long as
I can keep learning, I want to keep living. And if along the

way I can teach something of the power of God to the next generation, I'll count that as a bonus.

℘ 72.1,4

Give the King your justice, O God,
and your righteousness to the King's Son....
He shall defend the needy among the people;
he shall rescue the poor and crush the
oppressor.

The Jews' understanding of God had included from the beginning the notion that God has a preference for the powerless—the orphan, the widow, the stranger in our midst. Faithful living therefore included caring for the least among the people, and this responsibility fell not only upon individuals, but upon society as a whole, represented by the king. The king of Judah was accountable to God, and it was the special responsibility of the king to defend the needy against those who would take unfair advantage.

Accountability is seen differently in modern western democracies. Rulers are seen as accountable not to God, but to the people because it's the people who elect them—and people are sinners. Most people look out for themselves and let the next fellow look out for himself. They vote for candidates who appeal to their narrow prejudices and interests, and scoff at the notion that God charges society as a whole—which normally means the government—with the responsibility to defend the needy and rescue the poor. This is true even among many Jews and Christians. A poisonous individualism has infected our souls, leading us to set aside biblical principles and deny our accountability for one another—and to God.

❦ 72.10

The kings of Tarshish and of the isles
shall pay tribute,
and the kings of Arabia and Saba offer gifts.

This psalm's references to foreign rulers paying homage to the king make it a fitting psalm for the Epiphany, when the wise men visited the infant Jesus. Foreign rulers in biblical times were usually seen as enemies to be contained, by force if necessary, and there is some of that in this psalm. But the psalm's dominant imagery is not one of subjugation. The picture is mainly one of voluntary and joyful submission, by every ruler and nation, to the long awaited King.

A similar drama takes place within the soul of the faithful Christian. There may be no better list of the foreign powers within us than the Seven Deadly Sins of medieval moral theology: pride, envy, anger, sloth, avarice, gluttony, and lust. These forces seek to invade and capture our souls, refusing the lordship of Christ and the gentle moving of the Spirit, and they must be contained. Force is sometimes necessary, in the form of discipline. But the use of force can have the opposite effect, strengthening the enemy's hold over us. Voluntary and joyful submission is the better way. The Lord

Christ speaks tenderly to these inner foes which hold us in thrall, inviting them to surrender, lay down their arms, and bow before him. When they do, a soul is redeemed and there is rejoicing in heaven.

❧ 72.17

May his Name remain for ever
and be established as long as the sun endures;
may all the nations bless themselves in him
and call him blessed.

The coronation of a new king in ancient times, like the inauguration of a new President today, was a time of hope. A new era invites dreams that new leaders will find fresh solutions to old problems. This psalm was written for such an occasion.

Christians have long applied this psalm to the reign of Jesus Christ. Its vivid images suggest the universal reign of Christ, with all peoples and nations paying homage to the King of kings. The hope it expresses is not so much a hope for heaven as a hope that prosperity, justice, and peace will prevail in this world "from sea to sea" and "as long as the sun endures."

The daily headlines and newscasts seem to mock this hope. Prosperity, justice, and peace seem to move farther beyond reach every day. Are there realistic grounds for Christian hope? Yes, but do not look for them in the headlines and newscasts. Looking back into history can reveal progress in some areas and hence support a Christian hope for the future—diseases have been conquered; Nazism and Communism have fallen. But the best place to look is in smaller places, nearer to home, among ordinary people. Jesus Christ changes countless lives every day, bringing joy and peace to those who trust and follow him. The grounds on which Christian hope rests are found in the hearts of faithful people. Whether that hope someday becomes a reality in the world at large, we cannot now know. Christ does not call us to know, but to trust and to follow.

Book Three

☙

Psalms 73 through 89

In vain have I kept my heart clean,
and washed my hands in innocence.

Yes, the wicked prosper and are at ease—or at least they seem to be at ease, and virtuous living can seem like a stupid idea. In *The Beautiful Ones Are Not Yet Born*, by Ghanian novelist Ayi Kwei Armah, the main character is a railroad clerk who refuses to take a bribe, which is contrary to how business is done in the African setting where the novel takes place. His family does not respect him because he fails to provide for their needs, which they know he could if he played the game as others play it. He feels guilty and like a failure even while he tells himself he has done nothing wrong. His life seems futile and hopeless. "The foolish ones are those who cannot live life the way it is lived by all around them," the novel says, "those who will stand by the flowing river and disapprove of the current. There is no other way, and the refusal to take the leap will help absolutely no one at any time."

I think Armah disagrees with that statement, but when virtue seems to offer no rewards, it's a point of view that does cross the mind. I have never faced such a temptation. There is corruption and greed in America, but our judicial system and sense of public responsibility usually hold them in check. Moreover, I have always had enough earned income and savings to provide everything my family needed. But what if I had been poor and lived in a country where bribery and corruption were endemic—"Everybody does it; you're a fool if you don't"—and knew that if I didn't take the bribe, the next man would and then his children would receive the education and other advantages I was denying mine? I can't quite swallow the psalmist's solution to the problem—he finally came to believe that despite appearances, wrongdoers would come to ruin—because that's not what I see happening. I don't know the answer, nor do I know what I would have done had I lived my life in another place.

℘ 73.21

When my mind became embittered,
I was sorely wounded in my heart.

Years ago I became angry at pretty much the whole world, including its Creator. The only thing going my way was my salary, which was, at least by clergy standards, large. But my big paycheck didn't deliver any of the things a big paycheck is supposed to deliver. I was miserable. At work I felt unappreciated, manipulated, and abused. At home, my wife seemed unsympathetic. No one seemed to understand or care. Worst of all was the fact that God wouldn't even show his face when I called out to him. I saw myself as the innocent victim of a pernicious universe. The blame for my misery lay with others, I was sure, and I loved to draw up lists of the guilty parties, then fantasize about what I hoped would happen to them.

It took a career change and a move to another city before I came to see what had really been going on in my life. Like the psalmist, I was "sorely wounded in my heart," and while other people were not entirely blameless, many of my wounds were self-inflicted.

I had allowed myself to become embittered—and bitterness is always a choice. It's a choice Jesus did not make. If anyone had a right to become bitter, it was surely Jesus—has anyone ever been as "sorely wounded" in his heart as Jesus was? But Jesus did not choose bitterness. He actually prayed that his enemies be forgiven, and at the very moment he was dying a horrible death at their hands. I can now do the same with those at whom I was angry those many years ago. The astonishing thing about Jesus is that he didn't do it years later, but while he was still bleeding.

☙ 73.25

Whom have I in heaven but you?
and having you I desire nothing upon earth.

I'm not there, at least not yet. Oh yes, like the psalmist, I desire to know and adore the Lord in heaven. I long to stand before the heavenly throne and the Lamb, clothed in my white robe and waving my palm branch. I think often of heaven. But heaven feels elusive to me, out there somewhere, hoped for but hidden, as if in a fog. And unlike the psalmist, that's not all I desire. I desire things on earth, too.

My earthly desires have changed as I've grown older. Power and reputation no longer call out to me. I don't want more money or a bigger, better, or newer anything. I want to love and to be loved. I want to create and to contribute. I seek little things, common things. And most of all, I desire to know and love the Lord—on earth, here and now. I grieve when this seems more a wish for me than a present reality.

My knowledge of the Lord is halting, tentative. It comes and goes. I adore the little I know and the vastly more that I hope for, but I want such a rock-like faith that I may be lost in wonder, love, and praise, not merely when in heaven I take my place, but on earth, right here, right now.

I bring to you, Lord, what faith I have. Accept the gift I bring, for I have no other. Do with it as you will. Nourish my faith, if you will, that as it grows, I may come to praise you with a fuller heart and voice. But if not, then grant me sufficient glimpses of you as I travel this life, that I may never stray from you. And when I die, welcome me to heaven, that I may gaze at last upon your face.

❧ 74.15-16

Yours is the day, yours also the night;
you established the moon and the sun.
You fixed all the boundaries of the earth;
you made both summer and winter.

When we grow anxious about something, every moment can be consumed by the anxiety. With no energy or time left for God, we lose the sense of God's presence. When this begins to happen to me, I often turn to a passage like this one and make myself sit quietly and allow the lines of the psalm to seep through my soul.

The references in these verses to day and to summer suggest to me cheerful, confident times. God grants us such times and we can thank him for them. The "sunshine in the meadow" times, I call them. The references to night and winter, on the other hand, suggest fearful, lonely, tense times. God grants us—or allows us to undergo—times of this sort as well, and while I don't suppose he expects us to be grateful for them, many have found that God draws them closer to him during these times—when they pause and allow him to do so, which it takes quite a while for some people to do.

Both day and night, both summer and winter, both good times and bad belong to God. Everything is God's; he has established, fixed, made all things. Everything ultimately rests in him, including every human being and all the things we fret about. Even when we feel bereft and cut off from God, the reality is only that we cannot see God, not that he has withdrawn. The absence of God is merely a state of mind, not an objective fact.

℘ 74.19b

The dark places of the earth are haunts of violence.

Darkness is a common synonym for evil, as in the "Prince of Darkness," a name for the devil, or the phrase "the dark side" from the popular "Star Wars" movies. Night seems to energize the evil in us. It is in dark places that sleeping demons are most likely to awaken and seize the souls of the unwary. Drunkenness, despair, illicit sex, domestic violence, occult rituals—these evils most often beguile us in the darkness. Perhaps our lives seem most barren in the dark.

Darkness also affords a cloak to conceal what would shame or damn us if revealed in the daylight.

There are also dark places within us, some known to us but concealed from others, some unknown even to us. Anger, envy, vengefulness, self-pity, the judging of others—these passions often poison our souls in secret, lurking unseen, covered by a veneer of respectability. I write these words on the day before Advent, and I think of the collect we shall pray in church tomorrow, asking for grace to cast away the works of darkness.

But dark places can also be holy places—places of rest and renewal, of tenderness and intimacy, where gentle night breezes, crickets, and whippoorwills contribute to rather than detract from a sacred silence. Those who listen for the voice of God often hear God speaking in the night. In some African churches, all-night vigils are important occasions for celebrating the Lordship of Christ and bringing people to him. God will sanctify our darkness and fill our emptiness with his grace when we invite him in and surrender our darkest secrets to him.

ᘓ 75.2a

"I will appoint a time," says God.

Three- and five-year plans may have some value, but usually it's not much. Vestries of parishes I served often named long-range planning committees to look at program, staff, property, and financial projections and plan accordingly. I always suspected little would come of their meetings, and in most instances, so far as I could see, that was true. These efforts were largely futile because people either forgot about the plan later or became so committed to it that they were loath to change it when unforeseen events made the plan redundant or inoperable.

The value in these efforts, if there was one, was that they moved people to think about the future rather than the past, and adoring the past is the bane of many a Christian congregation. But it is God, not we, who determines the future, and God loves surprises. This psalm envisions a time when justice will be done on earth, when boasters will be knocked off their pedestals and the wicked will drink bitter wine. It is well to envision a time of justice, still better to work to bring it to pass. But we set ourselves up for repeated disappointments, possibly even complete disillusionment, if we draw up a timetable and measure the success of our efforts against it.

Faithful living has a tentative quality to it. We must do our best to anticipate and provide for the future, but always remember that what we anticipate may not come to pass, and if it does, it will almost certainly be with surprising twists. Each moment is a new revelation of the goodness and winsomeness of our unpredictable God. As someone once said to me, "If you want to make God laugh, tell him your plans!"

⌘ 76.1-2

In Judah is God known;
his Name is great in Israel.
At Salem is his tabernacle,
and his dwelling is in Zion.

Only in Judah? Only in Israel? Only in Jerusalem (Salem is an older form of the name Jerusalem) and on Mount Zion? Isn't that awfully exclusive? Isn't it presumptuous, and a little bit ridiculous? Do you mean the universal God, the Maker and Lord of all creation, is known *nowhere else?*

Well, yes, that's what pretty much we mean. It's an overstatement, but not much of one. It's not that God isn't present everywhere—he is, and the perceptive person can catch glimpses of his glory wherever and whenever. It is just that God has chosen a particular place to disclose himself most intimately and fully. You ask, why that place? Yes, one does wonder about that. There's no obvious reason why, of all the spots on earth, God would have chosen Jerusalem, and of all the peoples of the earth, God would have chosen that particular people. "How odd of God to choose the Jews," as someone once said. But then, that's not the only odd thing about God. In fact, God routinely fails to measure up to our definitions of what a decent and respectable deity should be. He won't stay put in heaven, surrounded by his angels and archangels where he can be properly adored. He's always fraternizing with his creation, and more often than not, with the least reputable parts of it, like the rag-tag bunch of nobodies through whom he chose to disclose himself to the world and eventually visit it in person. That's the scandal of Judaism, and even more the scandal of Christianity, that of all the things God could choose to do, he would chose to do that, and to do it there.

⚘ 77.3-4

I think of God, I am restless,
I ponder, and my spirit faints.
You will not let my eyelids close;
I am troubled and I cannot speak.

I made the most difficult decision of my life in the summer of 1994. I had been offered a position I would normally have accepted in a heartbeat. It entailed a large pay raise, challenging work I knew I'd enjoy, congenial colleagues, and an opportunity to relocate to a city I knew and loved. But the small parish where I was rector had begun to grow and was in the midst of a building campaign. To have left then, I felt certain, would have destroyed the parish's morale and momentum.

While I debated my decision in my mind, I spent many restless nights pondering God and his will for me. I felt like the rope in a tug-of-war game, pulled in two directions, taut and exhausted. When at last I turned down the job, a deep peace filled my soul. I relaxed and slept soundly for the first time in weeks. I knew I had made the right decision, and not for one moment have I regretted it.

My restlessness had resulted from my inability or unwillingness (I'm still not sure which it was) to hear what

God was saying to me. I had been weighing the reasons for and against the move, then assessing them as I would have added up the columns of a ledger sheet. I was listening for God only in my mind, with my rational and logical self. God was speaking, though, not in my mind, but in my heart. When I finally listened in my heart (it took a comment from my wife to get me to do it), I heard God's voice and yielded to him—completely, heart and mind, ego and will, every dream and every desire. Only then were my contentment and energy restored.

℞ 77.10

And I said, "My grief is this:
the right hand of the Most High has
lost its power."

In his book *Night*, Holocaust survivor Elie Wiesel recounts with gripping, understated intensity his experiences of being carried away as a young boy by the Nazis and the horrors that followed. He had been a devout child, intending one day to study for the rabbinate. Wiesel writes, "Never shall I forget that nocturnal silence that deprived me, for all eternity, of the desire to live. Never shall I forget those moments that murdered my God and my soul and turned my dreams to dust. Never shall I forget these things, even if I am condemned to live as long as God Himself. Never."

Had the Most High lost its power? Had God dozed off? Did God not care? Was God simply the devil by another name? Evil kills not only people—it kills the faith of those who remain alive.

I would never presume to advise a Holocaust survivor about matters of faith and meaning. But like many of them, I have at times suspected that God was helpless, absent, or an illusion. Two thoughts have eased the grief I felt on those occasions: First, the scriptures advise waiting upon the Lord. One can learn to wait. Perhaps if I wait patiently, God will lighten this darkness. I make myself recall earlier times when I believed, trusted God, and enjoyed God's fellowship, and I try to return to those times in my mind. Second, I think of Christ on the cross—God has in the past brought good out of evil, with astonishing results. Perhaps good will come of this present darkness. Perhaps it only appears that the Most High has lost its power.

Perhaps, perhaps, perhaps—and perhaps I am wrong. You cannot *know*. Faith is a choice, and never a sure one. The doubt, the mocking questions, the grey fog—these are part of grieving for a God who has lost his power or seems to have lost it. Could such grieving be part of faith?

ও 77.19b

...yet your footsteps were not seen.

It is the rare Christian who goes through life with an uninterrupted sense of God's presence. For most, that sense comes and goes. God is present, within us and around us, working his purposes, accomplishing his designs—but often we do not see him. Why not?

One reason, I suspect, is that God may not wish to be seen. "Absence makes the heart grow fonder," the maxim says. What is never denied can be taken for granted. If I hadn't known this before, I discovered it when I traveled to Africa for several months to teach theology. In 33 years, I had never felt so separated from my wife. Frequent emails made things somewhat better, but the depth of my longing for her astonished me. I sometimes ached to see her face and hear her voice. When I returned to America, I experienced a renewed love for her and a new appreciation for everything about her. God may have his reasons for not being perpetually visible at our side.

Another reason, surely, is that even when we might see God, we are so preoccupied with the petty concerns of the moment that we do not pause to look for him. Totally focused on what we want right now, we live as if under a tent, oblivious to God's hand at work in the world about us. Just as our ears are distracted by the constant noises in our lives, so that we cannot hear the voice of God in silence, our eyes are distracted by the glitter and clutter of things around us so that we cannot see God when he comes to us.

Lord, give us the assurance of things unseen, that we may always trust you, even when we do not sense your presence with us. Whether our failure to see you is of your own design or due to our clouded vision, carry us through, carry us all the way through, and bring us at the last to that place where your presence may so fill and encompass us that the shadows of doubt are reduced to mere memories and where you enable us to praise you with unveiled eyes and a grateful heart.

I will open my mouth in a parable;
I will declare the mysteries of ancient times.

Despite Jesus' fondness for parables, the notion that a parable can convey theology would once have seemed strange to me—theology was supposed to be contained in propositional statements beginning with such words as "God is..." Over the years, though, I have come to doubt the ability of human beings to make any definitive statements about God except for negative ones—God isn't this, God isn't that. But what about other sorts of language—poetry, biography, fantasy, song, parable? Might they offer possibilities for saying something more about God?

Matthew says that Jesus told parables "because seeing they do not see, and hearing they do not hear." (Mt. 13:13) That statement itself is harder to explain than most of Jesus' parables, so surely there was more to it than that. Jesus almost never explained a parable. He just told the story and let it hang there. People could do with it as they wished. That's the beauty of a story. If you tell a story to ten people, it will be ten different stories, because everyone will filter what she hears through her own personal life history; each listener will place herself into the story in a different way—and each way of hearing the story will be "true." The same can be said of other non-propositional forms of language.

I now believe that if we are to "declare the mysteries of ancient times" or speak of anything that really matters, it will have to be through a story or something like a story. Propositional statements just don't cut it. That's because propositional statements are static, whereas the things that really matter are all relationships—to God, to one another, to the rest of creation, to ourselves—and relationships grow and evolve. Stories grow and evolve, too. Their meaning changes as we change.

ℭ 78.6

That the generations to come might know,
and the children yet unborn;
that they in their turn might tell it to
their children.

"The young people aren't interested in church," we older people often say, shaking our heads sadly. It's true, at least in my denomination. The median age of the typical Episcopal congregation is 20 years higher than the median age of the U.S. population. Pentecostal and gospel rock churches may have more young people, but the church I love is gray-headed and wrinkle-faced, like me.

Is that a bad thing? Not necessarily. The fact that I love something doesn't mean it will or should stay around forever. I believe the Episcopal Church has a bright future, but denominations have their fat years and their lean years, and occasionally one has disappeared (usually by merging with another denomination), but God has carried on, and God will still carry on. I don't worry about it.

What does grieve me is that many in the younger generation seem not to know the scriptures as well as those who came before them. My grandparents, born in the 19th century, knew the Bible and taught it to me. That rarely happens these days, partly because grandparents don't live in the same communities as their grandchildren, and partly because when they do, they don't teach the Bible to them. Moreover, the increasing pluralism of the Western world and judicial rulings in America over the past half century have almost completely eradicated religious values from public life. Are the classic stories of God working in history to draw people into relationship to him going to be forgotten? Is the Bible going to become as unfamiliar to the typical American as Chinese history or African tribal legends? Are we junking the religious foundations of our civilization? Now *that* would bother me.

ℛ 79.5

How long will you be angry, O Lord?
  will your fury blaze like fire forever?

The situation that gave rise to this psalm was one of national catastrophe, the Babylonian invasion of Judah in 587 b.c. Everything the nation had held sacred and pinned its dreams on for 400 years was suddenly profaned and destroyed. Any people defeated militarily, especially if it is on their home turf, experiences similar feelings. Theologian William Porcher DuBose, who fought on the losing side in the American Civil War and whose home was burned to the ground by an invading army, wrote of his "sense of the utter extinction of the world."

Individuals can feel this way as well when relationships and institutions die or fail, or when forces, sometimes distant and impersonal, shatter their illusion of security. As the verse before this one makes clear, what is expressed here is more than grief. It has a dimension of humiliation to it, even of violation, of profanation. It is akin to being raped. And no one seems to care. Others merely scoff and deride the desolate.

The psalmist feels that God, who has at least allowed this to happen, perhaps even caused it, is angry with his people. He asks God to forgive his people and to redirect his anger towards the attackers. These are understandable sentiments. Even in the most horrible of tragedies God works through the events of our lives to draw us to him.

It is also true that God becomes angry and that penitence is often the right response to catastrophe. This does not mean, however, that God takes out his anger on disobedient people by bringing evil upon them. Nor does it mean that God approves of everything that occurs, still less that God directs it. When evil events occur, it is the devil who orchestrates them, not God. But God holds the trump card. In the end, God prevails, turning evil into good, defeat into victory, and humiliation into joy.

❧ 80.14

Turn now, O God of hosts, look down
from heaven;
behold and tend this vine;
preserve what your right hand has planted.

Written in response to the same national catastrophe that inspired Psalm 79, this is one of the Bible's most poignant expressions of confidence in God amidst devastating defeat. The psalmist sees God as the author of all things, even including the destruction of the nation. His relationship to God is intensely personal. He reminds God that God chose Israel, brought her out of Egypt and planted her as a vine in ground he had selected and prepared especially for her, then tended and nurtured what he had planted. Why has God now broken down the wall that protected his planting from wild animals? The psalmist appeals to God to remember and preserve the vine in which he has invested such love and care.

Would this have been a psalm which the Jews of the Holocaust would have prayed, or the American Indians, Armenians, Kulaks, Cambodians, Tutsis, Kosovars, or Sudanese—all victims of attempted genocide within the past century? Individuals who are abused, manipulated, or ravaged may have similar feelings. Would they pray this psalm? Sometimes all one can do is to call out to God and beg God to remember his goodness and his promises. God has not forgotten, of course, but in times of calamity, it may seem that God has forgotten, and to give voice to that sense of abandonment is not to be condemned.

Remember us, Lord, when we feel as if darkness has overcome light and our hope has been snuffed out. Remember your goodness of old. Preserve what your right hand has planted.

☙ 81.12-13

So I gave them over to the stubbornness
of their hearts,
to follow their own devices.
Oh, that my people would listen to me!
that Israel would walk in my ways!

Occasionally a passage of scripture gives us a glimpse into the heart of God. This psalm is such a passage. God is the speaker in much of the psalm, and the message is in the emotions conveyed by the psalm's tone and coloration, not in the words themselves. Just as in human language, the meaning is often conveyed more by facial expression, posture, and tone of voice than by the actual words. That's why a written transcript can miss entirely the import of the spoken word.

Although the parental metaphor is not explicitly stated, it underlies the entire psalm. The beloved child has turned his back on his parent. God has been abandoned by the one he loves; God is lonely; God grieves. At one moment, we hear God pleading with his child to listen, remember, and return to him. He would shower blessings upon his beloved, but the beloved wants none of it. In the next moment, we hear God doing what rejected mothers and fathers eventually must do—God agrees to let his child live its own life, make its own decisions, dance to the tune of its choosing, however destructive that dance might be.

But nothing can erase God's love. If our love for God is like a morning cloud, like the dew that goes early away, as Hosea says, God's love is a bottomless spring that never runs dry. God's undying love moved him, in the end, to try one more thing, a daring, unexpected, most ungodlike thing—God left the glory and splendor of heaven and went out in search of his beloved. God entered the wilderness of the lost, in person, in the flesh. And upon finding his beloved there, God claimed his beloved and brought his beloved home.

ᏬᎡ 82.1

God takes his stand in the council of heaven;
he gives judgment in the midst of the gods.

The original context of this psalm may have been the polytheistic culture of the ancient Middle East. Pagan deities, elsewhere in the Bible exposed as fake gods, are here envisioned as real gods, but deriving their authority from the God of Israel and accountable to him. We cannot prove even that there are other heavenly beings, much less know what characterizes the relationships among them. But this scene is tantalizing and suggestive.

Envision a courtroom in heaven. God is the supreme judge but a crowded court docket has caused God to delegate a number of cases to lower judges. God is now reviewing these cases, and he finds the other judges have violated the most basic principles of heavenly jurisprudence—they have favored the wicked. By taking the word of false witnesses? By accepting bribes? By winking at the misdeeds of their friends and relatives? We do not know how these lower judges have failed to do their duty, but their offense is serious enough that it has shaken the very foundations on which God established the earth (vs. 5). God is now holding these lower judges to account. Although they are "gods" and therefore presumably entitled to, or at least eligible for, immortality, it shall not be so. They are now sentenced to die as any earthly ruler would die (vs. 6-7).

Among the things this scene suggests are these:

Heaven isn't a static place where everything is always in good order. There is give and take there as well. Good and evil battle one another not only on earth, but throughout the created order, even in heaven.

The denial of divine justice affects more than the innocent victims. It shakes the very foundation of the God's creation.

God will hold those who pervert divine justice accountable.

ཙ 83.16

Cover their faces with shame, O Lord,
that they may seek your Name.

This is the only verse of this psalm that I like. Taken as a whole, the psalm is too bloody for me. Most of it is a lament over impending national catastrophe. The nation's enemies (these are also the enemies of God, of course) are plotting and planning dire things. Some ten nations are mentioned, all but the last of them (Assyria) small-fry tribes who are minor players on the international scene. But they intend havoc and are capable of it—yet the Lord seems unmoved. The psalmist recalls times past when the Lord wiped out similarly troublesome nations and appeals for a repeat performance.

Except for this verse (and perhaps verse 18), this psalm gives no hint that its author desired anything more than the total annihilation of these other nations. But here he suggests another motive for his prayer—that these other peoples may seek the Lord. The psalmist wants them to be shamed—and while shame usually leads to bitterness, hatred, and anger, it can, on occasion, lead to repentance and newness of life.

Nations at war and those intending war usually demonize their opponents. Public officials describe their enemies as evil and ruthless. But if you listen to the pronouncements of both sides, it's disconcerting how similar the voices are, regardless of whose leader is speaking. My guess is that all who castigate their enemies speak the truth because there is evil and ruthlessness on both sides. If the Lord is to punish the evil and ruthless, therefore, the punishment will be broadly meted out, and many who presume to speak on behalf of the

Lord will be caught by surprise when the punishment comes back on them. As I write, the world is at war, and the usual rhetoric is being heard from various capitals. Let us pray that when the punishment comes, as surely it will, it may lead our enemies and us not to hopelessness and bitterness, but to seek the Lord, for some, perhaps for the first time.

℃ 84.1a

How dear to me is your dwelling, O LORD of hosts!
My soul has a desire and longing for the
courts of the LORD.

When the parish where I was rector several years ago dedicated the new church we had built, the choir sang the famous setting of this text from Johannes Brahms' *A German Requiem.* The text is most appropriate for the dedication of a church. We speak of the church building as "God's house" and feel close to God in a church, perhaps because the architecture, art, and music suggest God's presence, or because the reason we go to church is to focus our thoughts on God.

But we also know, as Solomon did (I Kings 8:27), that no earthly building can contain God and that God dwells both within and beyond all buildings, places, and times. "Behold the heaven and the highest heaven cannot contain thee." There is no place and there is no moment, however dark or distant, in which God is not present.

As Christians, we believe God dwells in the hearts of people. Groups of Christians often speak of God's presence among them and individual Christians speak of God's presence within them. It is true that God may be among and within Christians. But if God is everywhere, may not God also be found among and within the unfaithful? Even where God is not acknowledged, where he is cursed, mocked, and derided, is he not present? No group of people and no individual is so foolish, wrong-headed, arrogant, malicious, frightening, blasphemous, or disillusioned that we cannot find God in them if we look for him. We have a choice. We can respond and relate to people on the basis of the evil we see in them, or on the basis of the good we see in them, faint though the light of that goodness may be. As we would wish others to relate to us, let us relate to them.

God calls out to us everywhere and from within the depths of every soul. We are to seek him in all his dwelling places, then make our home with him.

❧ 84.3

Happy are they who dwell in your house!
they will always be praising you.

The author of this psalm was a devout layman who composed these words in connection with a pilgrimage to the temple in Jerusalem. Clearly, he did not live there. We may assume that like most people in ancient times, he labored long hours at exhausting tasks to eke out a living for himself and his family. The journey to worship at the temple was probably a taxing one, a rare privilege, not often undertaken. The temple staff, the priests, on the other hand, lived in the temple or its environs. The psalmist fantasizes about the happiness of those who live every moment in the house of the Lord. They are able to praise him not just from time to time, when a pilgrimage becomes possible, but all the time. One day where they reside is better than a thousand elsewhere (vs. 9).

I have often wondered what notions modern lay people entertain about their clergy. Some clergy live in parsonages or rectories on the church grounds, as the ancient Jerusalem priests did, spending most of their time on church-owned property. Are they always praising God? Is one day in their quarters better than a thousand elsewhere? Well—that depends. If the laity assume their clergy are exempt from envy, disillusionment, vanity, and boredom, that they spend every moment in rapturous adoration of their Maker, let them think again. Most lay people are probably not so naive as to think that, but some of them do make unrealistic assumptions about their clergy.

Here's the truth: Beneath our fancy ecclesiastical attire, clergy are identical to lay people. Both groups do what they do for various reasons, some noble and some not so noble. We wrestle with the same temptations, coming up victorious about equally often. Those, lay or ordained, who have truly surrendered their lives and wills to God are blessed, happy. A day with them probably is better than a thousand days with someone else. But ordination has nothing to do with it.

℘ 85.10-11

Mercy and truth have met together;
righteousness and peace have kissed
each other.
Truth shall spring up from the earth,
and righteousness shall look down
from heaven.

Many people have a sense that the world is broken, that what was once right has gone tragically wrong. The classical doctrine of the Fall addresses this sense. It is as if people have a faint, not quite obliterated memory of a time when things now blurred were in focus, relationships now hostile were friendly, souls now soiled were clean. People long for things to be put right again, for what could and should be (and once was?) to become what is.

This psalm begins as a lament, bewailing God's apparent abandoning of his people. The psalmist begs for God to restore his people, to show mercy, to give life again. In the psalm's latter verses, he expresses confidence that his prayer will be answered, for "salvation is very near." Then comes a powerful, soaring image—spiritual virtues are personified and come together in a joyful, intimate reunion. Mercy, truth, righteousness, peace—we need not try to define these virtues or distinguish them from each other. These are not opposites being reconciled. Rather, these virtues, taken together, comprise a picture of the world as God intends it to be. Somehow, they have become estranged from one another, but in the psalmist's vision they are reunited. Heaven bows to earth and earth reaches up to heaven. The two meet, kiss, and become one. The petition in the Lord's Prayer that "thy will be done on earth as in heaven" becomes reality. The Fall is reversed.

The verb tense in these verses is uncertain. Various translators have rendered them in the past, present, and future tenses. It doesn't matter, because this is a vision of what God intends. Christians see God's intention acted out in our midst in the person of Jesus Christ, and we trust that the present and the future, despite current events that sometimes suggest otherwise, are in his hands.

❧ 86.11

Teach me your way, O LORD,
and I will walk in your truth;
   knit my heart to you that I may fear
    your Name.

This psalm has been called a collage. The psalmist borrows several phrases on related themes from other psalms and pastes them, as it were, onto his own canvas. These themes emerge at different points within the psalm, but there is little progression of thought within the psalm as a whole.

Verse 11 is, I believe, the pivotal verse. Enemies threaten the psalmist, and he has called to the Lord for help. Although he says he is faithful (vs. 2), he does not boast because he realizes his faithfulness is due not to his own insight, commitment, or courage, but to the power and goodness of God within him. He focuses on this experience of God rather than on his own troubles. This gives the psalm a confident, even joyful tone not found in other psalms of lament. The plaintive pleas, desperate sighs, and occasional wallowings in self-pity and vindictiveness which weigh down other such psalms are absent here. In verse 11, the psalmist asks for an additional gift of the blessing he has already received from the Lord.

The psalmist also realizes he needs more than "head knowledge" about God. He needs for God to "knit my heart to you." Other translations say "keep my heart steadfast in this one thing," "give me an undivided heart," and "make me single-hearted." It is one thing to have right ideas about God, to be clear in our theology and doctrinal positions, but that matters little unless our hearts are one with God. The collect for Proper 7 in the 1979 Book of Common Prayer could serve as a summary of this psalm: "O Lord, make us to have a perpetual fear and love of thy Name, for thou never failest to help and govern those whom thou hast set upon the sure foundation of thy loving-kindness."

❦ 87.3

I count Egypt and Babylon among those who know me;
behold Philistia, Tyre, and Ethiopia:
in Zion were they born.

Of the dozen or so psalms which extol the glories of Jerusalem and Mount Zion, this is one of the most perplexing and suggestive. If written after the return from the Exile (perhaps likely, but not certain) its several references to the faithful living in foreign nations may be meant to assure Jews scattered throughout the world that Jerusalem remained their true home. People living in a foreign land often continue to regard the country from which they came as their true home and cling to reminders of it. This can continue even after several generations among those who have no actual memory of that country but have been reared on stories handed down from those who came before them.

Another, more startling thought may lie behind the psalm as well. The references to other nations do not mention Jews living within their borders, and the wording of the psalm seems to suggest that foreign nations themselves, not merely resident Jews, were "born in Zion." The nations mentioned include traditional enemies of Israel (Egypt, Babylon, Philistia) as well as friendly nations that had become trading partners (Tyre and Ethiopia). If all these are numbered among the people of God, the psalm becomes one of the Bible's most forceful statements of universalism.

The psalm raises these questions for the modern reader: If foreigners are to enter the household of God, what does that say about what it is to be the "chosen" people and what are its implications for international relations today? What gifts and new understandings will the foreigners bring? How will their presence change the household? Will those already in the household have things to learn, adjustments to make, traditions to enlarge or change in order to receive them? And why do so many of these peoples remain even now on the outside?

❧ 88.11-13

Do you work wonders for the dead?
will those who have died stand up and give
you thanks?
Will your loving-kindness be declared in the
grave?
your faithfulness in the land of destruction?
Will your wonders be known in the dark?
or your righteousness in the country where
all is forgotten?

No. Clearly, that is the implied answer to these searing rhetorical questions. This psalmist did not believe in an afterlife—of heavenly bliss, hellish torment, or anything else. Until very late in their history, the ancient Jews gave little thought to an afterlife, and when they did, they envisioned it as a dim, shadowy sort of half-existence. Life here and now was rich with meaning, but for its own sake, not because it was a prelude to what came afterwards. For many Christians, however, the next life is a key element of their faith, *the* key element for some. There is nothing wrong in this, but a narrow preoccupation with getting to heaven can distract us from the place where we must find and serve God. This world, after all, is where the Son of God lived and where we meet him.

Its tortured expressions of grief and dereliction give this psalm its power. Whether metaphorical or factual, its images—crying out day and night, lying in the pit, overcome by waves, darkness his only companion—tend to stick in the mind.

And there is one other thing: The psalmist consistently attributes everything that happens to him, grim as it may be, to the hand of the Lord. It is the Lord who has laid him in the abyss, sent great waves upon him, and put his friends far from him. It is the Lord who has rejected and terrorized him. But still he calls out to the Lord. He doesn't ask to be saved in heaven, or even that his enemies on earth be smitten. He asks merely to be heard, to be acknowledged. Circumstances which would have decimated the faith of others here produce a remarkable humility, patience, and acceptance.

ଓଃ 88.14-15

But as for me, O LORD, I cry to you for help;
in the morning my prayer comes before you.
LORD, why have you rejected me?
why have you hidden your face from me?

This psalm is a series of impassioned statements, questions, and metaphors about the psalmist's sense of abandonment by God. He feels isolated and derelict and pleads unremittingly to God for relief. The psalmist mentions only two outward things that trouble him, his rejection by former friends (vss. 9, 19) and failing eyesight (vs. 10), and even these words may be metaphors for spiritual abandonment. A friend of mine has called verse 14 "the epitome of faith."

The psalmist is experiencing what is called the "dark night of the soul." The phrase was first used by the 16th century Spanish mystic, John of the Cross. He didn't mean merely a dreary or difficult time (though others have since used the expression with that meaning). The dark night is not a time of pain, but a time of *nothing*. It is an emptiness created by God because of his love for us, in order that he may fill it with himself. It is also a great blessing. As earthly attachments and consolations are removed, the dark night begins to liberate, purify, and enlighten. As T. S. Eliot said, "Let the darkness come upon you which shall be the darkness of God." Or as Thomas Merton said, "The way that leads through dread goes not to despair but to perfect joy, not to hell but to heaven."

Since earthly consolations are shown to be inadequate and taken from us during the dark night, it is also a time of attack on conventional religion. Our relationship to God is reduced to its bare bones: What do we really seek? Spiritual comfort? Mystical highs? Inner peace? A sense of security? Reassurance about the future or the next life? These are all less than God. When they are removed, when even our belief in a God defined by traditional teachings and concepts is taken away, the result is a space for the real God to enter and fill. If this psalmist has not yet arrived at that place, he is very nearly there.

৫ 89.5a

The heavens bear witness to your wonders,
O LORD.

I recall as a young child gazing up at the Milky Way one night. I sensed the wonder and grandeur of God, surrounded by heavenly beings who praised and served him—"all the fire-folk sitting in the air! The bright boroughs, the circle-citadels there!" as Gerard Manley Hopkins said. Years later, after lots of educating, I still marveled at the Milky Way, but I wasn't so sure about God, and the thought of heavenly beings had come to seem a bit foolish. The only thing I was sure of was that the heavens contained vast numbers of atoms, most of them very hot, and vast expanses of emptiness, most of it very cold. A spectacular sight, yes—but "fire-folk sitting in the air?"

Children may be onto something. They don't assume as much as adults do. Adults, especially those of us trained in Western empiricism and the scientific worldview, want verification before we believe; we assume that if something is real, we must be able to find it, measure it, and analyze it. This eliminates fairies, guardian angels, the devil, and God. What a dull universe! Children, on the other hand, believe in things invisible and unknowable. Their universe includes mystery and wonder, even "fire-folk sitting in the air." It is not dull.

The Christian story is easier for children to accept than for adults. An invisible and unfathomable reality which, by startling choice and miraculous design, "came down from heaven" and assumed the form of human flesh? A God who not only disclosed himself to his creatures, but joined them, who not only creates, loves, and acts in his world, but who also, once upon a time, actually visited it in person, with astonishing consequences? A stunning reversal, at one minute before midnight, of what had seemed to be a lost cause? When you hear the story, if you don't quite get it, ask a child.

The heavens bear witness to your wonders,
O Lord,
and to your faithfulness in the assembly of
the holy ones;
For who in the skies can be compared to the Lord?
who is like the Lord among the gods?
God is much to be feared in the council of the
holy ones,
great and terrible to all those round about him.

The Bible calls heavenly beings by many names. "Holy ones" and "gods" refer to such beings in this psalm, but in modern parlance, we usually call them all angels. Angels are popular these days. Bookstores prominently display texts about angels. Angelic faces adorn coffee mugs. Angel magnets hang on refrigerator doors. Everyone seems to love angels. But many of these angels seem unrelated to God. They are cute and pretty, but what have cute and pretty to do with God?

Biblical angels are neither cute nor pretty. Like all biblical authors (but unlike some modern people), the psalmist assumed the reality of heavenly beings. This psalm's references to heavenly beings do not even hint at cute or pretty—they are about power and submission to power. Heavenly beings are servants of the Lord of the universe, and even they are terrified in the presence of God.

Angels often appear in the Bible as God's messengers, sent from heaven to earth. An angel comes at people from an unknown realm and challenges them with inconceivable thoughts and unconventional demands. Angels strike terror into those who encounter them. Typically, the first words a biblical angel speaks to someone are, "Don't be afraid!" I am certain the psalmist did not think of these heavenly messengers as models for decorative figurines.

❧ 89.19a

You spoke once in a vision...

The verses following this one suggest that the vision referred to is that of the prophet Nathan, spoken of in II Samuel 7, in which the Lord establishes the Davidic monarchy. This is not the only instance in the Bible where God speaks through a vision, but such things are rare. Normally, God speaks through historical events and the words of prophets. But those to whom a vision of God is granted never forget it.

I had a vision of God once. It took place on a gray, winter afternoon in Gambier, Ohio, 40 years ago and remains the single most compelling and memorable event of my life. It was a totally private event, occurring within me, perceived by no one else. I had no sense of its duration; it could have lasted a second or an hour. I only know where I was standing when it ended and that afterwards I knew that I, together with all the universe, was held in the loving arms of Jesus Christ.

For years, I told no one of this vision. To this day, I speak of it rarely, because when I do, I am usually met with blank stares, as if I'd said, "I ran into Henry VIII in the post office this morning." I too have wondered about my experience on that gray afternoon. Could it have been a hallucination? Something I ate? Call it what you wish—I shall never forget the power of that moment.

God does communicate through visions, but only to some people, and very rarely. Perhaps that's because visions, being easily misunderstood and fabricated, are dangerous things. The test of authenticity for any vision is this: Was it merely a thrilling moment, or are you more like Christ for having seen it?

Book Four

❦

Psalms 90 through 106

❧ 90.4

For a thousand years in your sight are like
yesterday when it is past
and like a watch in the night.

Given the age of the universe, usually put at 15 to 20 billion years, or even the length of recorded human history, about 6,000 years, a single human life is very brief. We are captives to the age in which we live. Bound by the customs and perspectives of our own time, none of us is capable of more than a very limited understanding of things. That is why the study of history and the reading of literature from earlier times is valuable—it removes us from our own time, mentally transporting us to a place where customs and perspectives differ from our own. That's where we are most likely to learn and grow.

God, on the other hand, does not need to learn and grow. God is not bound by time. God sees past, present, and future in a single glance. I like to think of time as a yardstick placed on the floor. We live our lives within a fraction of an inch on that yardstick, say, between inches 19 and 20. But of course we don't know the duration of history, so we can't be sure where on the yardstick any particular life falls. Whether we live near the beginning or near the end of time we cannot know. God, however, stands above the yardstick, gazing down at it. In a single moment, he takes in all of time— past, present, and future. All times are present to God.

The new physics has challenged the traditional conception of time and given us tantalizing new ways to conceptualize both time and eternity. The one thing it teaches us for sure is that there is more to the cosmos God has created than the human mind can encompass. We must reconsider much, perhaps everything, that once seemed beyond question. But Christians (unlike Buddhists) cannot completely abandon the notion of time as traditionally conceived. That is because, whatever else God may be and do, we believe he has acted *within* time, even entered it and subjected himself to it. It is primarily within history, not in speculative or mystical flights, that God makes himself known.

ॐ 90.5-6

You sweep us away like a dream;
we fade away suddenly like the grass.
In the morning it is green and flourishes;
in the evening it is dried up and withered.

Unlike most children, I thought a lot about death as a youngster, perhaps because I lived near lots of aged relatives. Death frightened me. The pain of dying did not frighten me, but I saw death, despite the church's teaching about heaven, as the threat of nothingness, non-existence. That still frightens me. Some people try to defeat the threat of nothingness by leaving a lasting mark behind them, but death is not so easily defeated. We are, as this psalm says, like the desert grass that springs up after an early rain but withers in the noonday sun and is gone by nightfall. Immortality is not a human attribute.

This realization can lead to one of two responses. One

is cynicism, perhaps even despair. If nothing lasts, one might say, then nothing matters. Do whatever gives you pleasure. Take what you want. Live it up while you can because that's all there is.

Others hear and respond to a voice from beyond this passing world. Sometimes I can hear this voice calling to me: "I don't ask you to make a mark in the world, that your name be known by future generations; I ask that you love me. I am the door, I am the way. Enter and follow. Follow me in the present moment. Do not ask whether those who come after you will remember your faithfulness. It matters not what will be said of you tomorrow. I will be with you tomorrow, as I am with you today. What matters is that you love and follow me today."

❧ 91.3-4

He shall deliver you from the snare of the hunter
and from the deadly pestilence.
He shall cover you with his pinions,
and you shall find refuge under his wings;
his faithfulness shall be a shield and buckler.

The first two verses of Psalm 91 are written in the third person, but verse 3 switches to the second person, suggesting an intimacy and immediacy not found in the opening two verses.

Four images give unusual power to verses 3 and 4. While the images are concrete and refer to actual physical dangers (and may well have been so understood by the psalmist), they can be read as metaphors for spiritual dangers without doing violence to the meaning of the text. I am reminded of *The Pilgrim's Progress*, John Bunyan's classic allegory in which he uses images of physical peril to discuss dangers to the soul.

The four images all pertain to God's love and care. They complement each other. The first is that of a snare set by a hunter or fowler to catch game. It suggests a rescuer reaching down by hand to pluck a victim out of a trap. The second is that of a deadly plague and the healing, medicinal or otherwise, which restores the sufferer to health. The third image is the most intimate, and my favorite of the four. A pinion is part of a bird's wing. The picture is that of a mother bird gathering her little ones close to her, where they can hear her heartbeat, feel the expansion of her lungs, and warm themselves next to her body, as tender and intimate a picture of loving care as I can imagine. The final image is a military one, an effective contrast to the gentleness of the preceding image. The shield is a large, heavy safeguard, protecting most of the body from danger but difficult to move; the buckler is a smaller, lighter piece, attached to the forearm, easily and quickly moved to deflect an arrow coming from an unanticipated direction. Together, shield and buckler constitute complete protection for a foot soldier.

❧ 91.5-6

You shall not be afraid of any terror by night,
nor of the arrow that flies by day;
Of the plague that stalks in the darkness,
nor of the sickness that lays waste at
mid-day.

Many people experience a restless, unfocused anxiety that consumes both day and night. I have experienced it myself on occasion.

Terror by night: Unknown, unseen threats cause me to wrench in my bed while the sun is still far below the eastern horizon. My mind hovers over the destruction, disappointment, rebuke, embarrassment, failure, humiliation, exposure which the coming day might bring. Does unanticipated rejection lurk behind the smiling faces of those whom I shall see tomorrow? What spiteful intentions do those smiles conceal? I also brood over yesterday's defeats—the broken promises, the broken relationships, the broken dreams. And what of the darkness within me? The deepest night, the most malevolent evils, are concealed in the crevices of my own heart.

The arrow that flies at mid-day: The sun is now in the top of the sky, and I am so busy with the telephone, the computer, my appointment book, and trips to and from the hospital, the bank, the store, and parishioners' homes that I forget why I do any of this. I'm going through the motions, the same motions I went through yesterday, and the day before, and the day before. God? At most, God is a dim flicker in the corner of my eye, easily ignored in favor of the pressing business in front of me.

Both day and night are in God's hands. Sometimes the things we dread do come to pass, but often they do not. We tend to dwell upon the worst of the possibilities the future may hold. Even when real pain and defeat come upon us, however, God is with us. Unlike our human acquaintances, God will never abandon us. His loyalty is beyond question, and he will sustain us.

❧ 91.7-10

A thousand shall fall at your side
and ten thousand at your right hand,
>   *but it shall not come near you.*
Your eyes have only to behold
>   *to see the reward of the wicked.*
Because you have made the LORD your refuge
>   *and the Most High your habitation,*
There shall no evil happen to you,
>   *neither shall any plague come near your*
>   *dwelling.*

I have heard these verses called "the ultimate soaring height of faith," a bold embrace of divine miracle that banishes all doubts and questions. Well, I don't think so. These verses are difficult for me. I can't see that they solve any problems; in fact, they create problems. They simply do not stack up against my experience. Bad people do not always get sick and die;

good people sometimes do get sick and die. God's protection is not a kind of insurance policy against adversity—or if it is, it doesn't work. Not only do these verses contain a naive view of suffering, but they can lead to disillusionment (when we've been good but we suffer nonetheless) or triumphalism (when we don't suffer and we assume it's because we've been good).

Two thoughts come to my mind: First, God's protection, though not an insurance policy against adversity, can make a positive difference in how we handle adversity. And second, while evil seems to afflict people indiscriminately, regardless of their faith or lack of it, I believe that *ultimately*, "no evil shall happen to you," that *ultimately*, God redeems all things, that *ultimately*, Jesus is King of kings and Lord of lords. I can't prove it by experience, but I believe it. I see hints of it now and then, but it's an act of faith. I *choose* to believe it.

ભ 92.1a

It is a good thing to give thanks to the LORD.

The U.S. Postal Service receives thousands of letters addressed to Santa Claus each year *before* Christmas, but only two or three *after* Christmas. The prayers of Christians addressed to God are much the same. We ask for things—healing, a better marriage, a good job, protection from danger, whatever—but when our requests are granted, we often go our merry way and give God hardly another thought. In America, we even have a holiday set aside for the purpose of giving thanks, but we usually observe it by eating a lot of food, watching football games, and preparing to invade the shopping malls the next day. The giving of thanks, if it happens at all, takes the form of a few sentences uttered as a table grace before the meal is eaten.

It is a good thing to give thanks to the Lord, the psalmist says. Why is that a good thing?

Giving thanks reminds us that everything we are and have is a gift. Life itself, the air we breathe, the space we occupy, the work we do, the people we know and love, our thoughts and dreams—it's all a gift. We didn't earn it; we didn't even inherit it from someone else who earned it. It comes to us from God, and nothing required God to give it to us.

Giving thanks humbles us. Acknowledging that everything is a gift leads to the question (so often posed by the psalmists with a different meaning), "Why me?" Baseball broadcaster Jack Buck said, shortly before his death, that if he could ask God one question when he got to heaven, it would be, "Why were you so good to me?" The answer has nothing to do with us and arises solely out of God's mysterious goodness. Knowing that punctures our puffed up pride.

Giving thanks takes us out of ourselves. The happiest people I know are those who focus their energies on someone or something beyond themselves. Some things we devote our energies to—getting more money, a more distinguished reputation, or a better high—may appear to take us beyond ourselves but are actually forms of self-obsession. Real thanksgiving leads to generosity, sharing, and a concern for others.

໕ 93.2

*He has made the whole world so sure
that it cannot be moved.*

I write these words a few months after the September 11 terrorist attacks on the United States.* War also appears possible at this time between India and Pakistan and between Israel and any of several Arab nations. The Iraqi government is, almost certainly, collecting an assortment of grisly weapons, and the U.S. government is making noises about invading Iraq. The "new world order" foreseen by the first President Bush is nowhere in sight. But then, dangerous times are nothing new, and these are not even the worst of times. So here comes this psalmist with his breezy assurance that God has established a world of unshakeable order. Oh, really?

Three responses come to mind. First, one could say, "Yes, but with my limited human vision, I can't see everything. There is order beyond what I can see."

Second, one could say, "Yes, things are chaotic, but there are also hints of lasting values and truths." At another time, I would have given each of those responses, and I suspect there is truth in both of them.

Now, however, as I approach old age, I lean towards a third response to the psalmist: "No, God has not made the world so sure that it cannot be moved—and I'm glad he hasn't." People have always longed for a sense of permanence,

*Editor's note: although written prior to war in Iraq, the author's words are addressing the point.

and while that is understandable, the fact is that nothing in this world is permanent—and that's a good thing. A stable, changeless world would lack opportunities for personal growth, fresh learnings, and new relationships. In a world where everything happened as it should, there would be no need of forgiveness, reconciliation, generosity, kindness, or compassion. With no wrongs to set right, no perplexing questions to probe, no noble endeavors to undertake, no chance for a new start after failure, would life be worth living? I am reminded of a comment by Vida Scudder: "Evil? I welcome it. For I think it is waking us up."

⋘ 94.17

If the LORD had not come to my help,
I should soon have dwelt in the land
of silence.

Most of this psalm is an appeal to God to set the world right, particularly to knock down the arrogant and insolent, and a series of derisive questions addressed to the offenders. Only in the concluding three verses do we discover the grounds for the psalmist's hope: When evildoers attacked him in the past, God has rescued him; his hope rests on personal experience.

There are always many ways to interpret a past event. When Moses led the Israelites through the Red Sea to safety from the Egyptian army, one might reasonably have attributed the event to Moses' gifted leadership, the stupidity of the Egyptians, or a fortuitous change in the wind direction.

There was no way to "prove" the interpretation the Israelites put on the event, that "the Lord brought us out of Egypt with a mighty hand." Faith cannot be demonstrated. It is a way of seeing things, an act of trust, a commitment. Chemical dependents learn this when they enter recovery. For 20 years, I have been a recovering alcoholic. People sometimes say to me, "It must have taken great willpower for you to conquer your drinking problem." That's a reasonable interpretation on the part of someone looking on from the outside. But every recovering person knows otherwise. If willpower could have prevailed, I would today be a moderate social drinker—God knows I tried that enough times! No, when I look back on the events that led me into recovery, I could paraphrase the ancient Israelites and say, "The Lord brought me out of slavery with a mighty hand."

This psalmist, it seems, had experienced a deliverance from some bondage or danger that he could only attribute to the direct intervention of God. It is on those grounds, the grounds of personal experience, that he trusts in the power of God to conquer and heal in the future and that he ventures to call upon God once more to "show yourself."

∽ 95.1-2

Come, let us sing to the LORD;
let us shout for joy to the Rock of our
salvation.
Let us come before his presence with thanksgiving
and raise a loud shout to him with psalms.

The opening verses of this psalm are a call to worship. It was presumably sung in procession at the Jerusalem temple, and it serves much the same purpose today in the Anglican service of Morning Prayer or Mattins. The reasons the psalmist gives for urging the people to worship are mainly the Lord's sovereignty over the whole earth—caverns, hills, seas—although the Lord's choosing and shepherding of Israel is also mentioned in verse 7. The worship enjoined is to be exuberant—worshipers are twice enjoined to *shout* their praises.

I wonder about all this shouting. Was the psalmist referring to something he experienced in worship, or urging on the people something different from their custom? Anyone who ponders the sovereignty of God deep within his heart will feel like shouting for joy, and worship in some places and denominations includes spontaneous outbursts. I have shouted during worship among Anglicans in Africa and in Pentecostal services in America. The same kind of thing occurs at athletic contests when the stands are filled with partisans. The emotional release afforded by shouting, whether at the ballpark or in church, can be riveting and cleansing of the soul. Was this the psalmist's experience in worship?

But when prayers and songs become familiar from many repetitions, worshipers can take them for granted, mumbling the words, or declining even to speak them at all. Tepid faith can produce the same thing. Dull, drab worship, for whatever cause, is like walking into a once grand hotel which has not been maintained and is now soiled and threadbare. Was this the psalmist's experience in worship?

Given a choice, I'd side with the psalmist in favor of shouting.

℘ 95.9-10

They put me to the test,
   though they had seen my works.
Forty years long I detested that generation...

These verses (beginning with the last line of verse 7) serve as a warning to the people not to repeat unacceptable behaviors practiced by those who came before them. The reference is to Exodus 17, where despite the Lord's providential care of the Israelites in the wilderness, their chronic belly-aching leads Moses to name the place Meribah (contention) and Massah (testing).

The Lord "detested" that generation, says the psalmist. The word detested is a strong word, but an accurate translation of the Hebrew. Other modern translations say that the Lord "loathed" or was "indignant," or "repelled" or "disgusted" by that generation. The King James Version says the Lord "grieved" with them. Clearly, more was involved than merely breaking a rule, even a sacred rule. The Lord's response was less like that of a judge sentencing a criminal guilty of multiple offenses than that of a parent confronting a child who had repeatedly flouted the parent's guidance. God takes the Israelites' misbehaviors *personally*.

The Bible's God, unlike the gods of the philosophers and of most other religions, is intensely personal. He (not It) enters into relationships, is offended, pleased, angered, amused, does things, even changes his mind occasionally. But does the God of the Bible actually *detest* people when they turn their back on him? Elsewhere the Bible suggests otherwise. Amos (5:21-24) says the Lord hates superficial acts of worship, but not the worshipers themselves. Hosea (11:1-9) portrays the Lord as unable to turn against his people, despite their corrupt ways, because of his long-standing devotion to them. And Isaiah (55:8-9) assures us that God's thoughts are not our thoughts, his ways not our ways. The psalmist is using hyperbole to make the point that our unfaithfulness is more than wrong behavior—it wounds the very heart of God.

☙ 96.6

Oh, the majesty and magnificence of his presence!
Oh, the power and the splendor of his
sanctuary!

Where is God? Where is his sanctuary? God had manifested himself in various guises—in a dream to Joseph, as fire and smoke to Moses, as a voice to Samuel and Elijah, as a boiling pot to Amos, as a heavenly vision to Isaiah and Ezekiel, as a tornado to Job. God had also spoken to his people through human devices—churches and temples, laws and ordinances, sacred texts, art, music, occasionally even sermons. And of course God had disclosed himself through other people, in the form of the redeeming word, the healing touch, the forgiving embrace.

But none of these proved adequate. People might have known by such means what they were to do, even that they mattered to another person. And they might have learned something about God. But God still seemed remote, like someone sending a message to them through an emissary, a third party, while God himself stood far off, safely distant.

How would we relate to such a God? Could a God like that really understand the world in which he has placed us, the uncertainties, fears, and tragedies we confront every day of our lives? Could such a God truly *love* us? We could not know for sure. So long as God merely disclosed his power, beauty, and goodness from a distance—"in light inaccessible, hid from our eyes"—we might fear or admire God, but we could never know that God loved us. And so God tried something new, something radical, something risky. He came to join us himself, in person, in the flesh. God entered a new sanctuary, a habitation he shares with us, constructed of achy joints and tired backs, sweaty armpits and bleeding wounds, subject to misunderstanding, jealousy, pain, and betrayal. It began in a manger and ended on a cross.

At last, God is with us. At last, we know God loves us.

෬ 96.9a

Worship the LORD in the beauty of holiness.

The English word holy translates the Hebrew *qodesh*, which means set apart or different. Only God is pure holiness, "absolutely other," as a professor of mine used to say. We experience God's total otherness as mysterious, powerful, and strangely alluring, but we can say nothing of God other than negatives—God is *not* this, *not* that—because anything positive we might say of God would imply that he is like us in some way, using words that derive from human experience. Human language lacks the capacity to define, even to approach, the "absolutely other." Certain places, persons, and objects are also looked upon as holy, but in a derivative sense, secondarily, solely because of their association with God.

Beauty and holiness are closely linked. Churches are deemed holy places, and they are often beautiful. The parish I served during the 1990s constructed a new church. The architectural lines, windows, floor finishes, metals and fabrics were selected for more than their utilitarian value. Great care went into creating a space suggesting something radically different from the world outside. A window was seen as more than something to provide light or to look through; a floor, more than something to walk on. The beauty with which we adorn our churches is intended to say that the God worshiped there is *holy*.

There is nothing wrong in this. But we are sometimes tempted to reduce the beauty of holiness to mere aesthetics or good taste. The prophet Amos (5:21-24) reminds us that the Lord despises worship that is merely elegant. If holiness is aesthetic, it must also be moral; if it is pretty, it must also be just. What makes a place holy is not its visible charm, but that acts of obedience and adoration occur there, that hearts are converted and lives transformed there, that inequity and anxiety give way to justice and peace there. Ultimately, our worship must make our lives holy, so that every thought and deed, whether inside or outside the church building, manifests the beauty of holiness.

℘ 97.2a

Clouds and darkness are round about him.

When teaching about faith in God, I have sometimes introduced a group of students to the blind man's game. One person is blindfolded while another gives directions: "Walk straight ahead. Now turn left. Feel for the table ahead of you. Reach for the bannister on your right, then walk down the stairs." The blindfolded student must believe that the person speaking will not cause her to bruise her shin on a coffee table or tumble down a flight of stairs. She must learn to trust.

Obeying God is like playing the blind man's game. It's often hard to do. The voice of God is not always easily heard. On the few occasions when I have asked God for guidance when facing a major decision, I heard not a word, not a hint of a word. It felt as if God had left me alone to make the decision by weighing the factors pro and con and wrestling with my personal values—by the seat of my pants, as it were. At other times, the apparent victory of evil in the world makes belief in a good, strong, and reliable God seem ludicrous to me—if there is such a God, why do I see neither him nor any evidence of him? Clouds and darkness envelop God; faith becomes a leap into the dark. I have decided to trust the hints of God I do see now and then, though there is always the possibility that I could be mistaken about them.

God could, presumably, have revealed himself unambiguously. It would have made life easier, eliminating the need to ask questions, evaluate situations, and make difficult decisions. With the meaning and purpose of life completely and undeniably clear, all possibility of doubt and skepticism removed, we could simply program ourselves to do the right thing. Why did God not make a world like that? Perhaps questioning, struggle, growth, and faith—leaping into the dark—are integral to his design. I suppose that in heaven, where the redeemed will stand before the throne of God, this will no longer be the case. Sometimes I'd like a moment like that now.

⚘ 98.1

Sing to the LORD a new song,
for he has done marvelous things.

Now let me see—how many kinds of noisy praise are mentioned in these 13 verses? People singing, that's one. Shouting, that's two. Then harps, trumpets, and horns. Then roaring seas, lands (earthquakes? rockslides?), clapping rivers, and ringing hills. That's nine altogether. It's not clear just what the Lord has done to elicit this superfluity of praise—a deliverance from some danger or oppression, probably—but it's clear that everyone and everything is to join in, including all people, both friends and enemies (vs. 8), fields and trees (vss. 11-12), even bodies of water and land formations (vss. 8-9). Things not mentioned are omitted, I suppose, for lack of space. The sound of it all would be—well, I can't imagine what it would be.

This is not the only place in the Psalter where non-human voices are bidden to join human voices in praising their Maker. Psalms 96 and 148 are similar to this one, and Psalm 19 invites the days and nights to proclaim the glory of God to each other. I suppose we must regard this language as metaphorical. Surely the psalmist didn't actually believe plants and rocks and bodies of water could praise God.

Or did he? I am aware, from my travels and my reading, of the myriad ways in which human beings praise God. Anyone who believes God is glorified with only one sort of music or prayers in only one idiom has just not been paying attention to what's going on. Then there are acts of kindness and sacrifice—surely these are means of praising God. There are probably angels in heaven who praise God in some other way. I saw a column of ants this morning as I was saying my prayers on my porch. They were traipsing a distance of about 60 feet from their home to a large tree, then back again, for what purpose I don't know. But I'm sure I heard them praising God as they scampered along. Isn't it possible that every created thing, every atom, every galaxy, everything everywhere joins in its own way to praise its Maker?

❧ 99.1a

The LORD is King;
let the people tremble.

Hold the first line of this psalm up against the first line
of Psalm 97: "*The Lord is King; let the people rejoice.*" Okay,
the Lord is King—so how should we respond? Should we
tremble or rejoice? Or sometimes one, sometimes the
other? Or both simultaneously? Or is it trembling for some,
rejoicing for others? What gives here?

Paradox, incongruity, ambiguity—that's what gives
here. Sometimes I think that's about all there is to life: From
solitude, community emerges. We live in the present while we
anticipate the not yet. The world's wisdom is God's foolishness; the world's foolishness is God's wisdom. In surrendering
ourselves, we discover who we are. When we stop demanding
what we want, we receive what we never knew to ask for. The
active life is nourished by solitude. In dying, we live. The cross
stands radiant against the sky. Paradox after paradox after
paradox.

Despite our rebellion, the Lord is King. Despite our
abuse of his creation, the Lord is King. Despite our attempts
to play God, the Lord is King. We rejoice in this, and at the
same time we tremble.

In my youth, I expected things to make sense. I
no longer do. Life is not a mathematical equation which
balances neatly once it is solved—life is always out of balance, it is never "solved." Paradox, incongruity, and ambiguity
are not exceptions to the norm—they *are* the norm. They
are not aberrations to be fixed, but part of the basic fabric

of the universe. Holding opposites together in tension, neither sinking into despair on the one hand, nor escaping into denial on the other, is perhaps what faithful living means. But whatever it means, and even if we haven't a clue what it means, the Lord is King.

☙ 100.3c

Give thanks to him...

Thank you, Lord, for sharp cheddar cheese, Bellingrath Gardens, a good night's sleep, that I have learned to take my opinions less seriously as I've grown older, the absence of the designated hitter in the National League, Bill Wilson and Doctor Bob, parishioners who've forgiven my foibles and helped me grow beyond them, winter wind and summer sunshine on my cheek, maps and atlases, onions, the Body and Blood of Christ given for me;

Four Brahms symphonies, windows that can be thrown open at night, Isaac Watts and Charles Wesley, friends who love me enough to confront me with the truth I'd rather ignore, shoes that fit just right, Doonesbury, strong black coffee, Feodor Dostoyevsky, the sound of a pipe organ echoing through a vast church, my three sons and the pleasure they give me, mangoes right off the tree, front porches with swings, people who pick up the trash, coffee mugs, Augustine of Hippo, bright neckties, children who come to communion with hands outstretched, biblical characters in whom I see something of myself—Abraham, Hezekiah, Nicodemus, Thomas, and Gamaliel;

Aspirin, milkweed pods that explode in the fall with a thousand silky seeds, oatmeal creme pies, the feeling in my chest after I have run and showered, work I love when some lack work and some hate theirs, Samuel Johnson, my parents' faith in God and in me, the memory of being afraid or depressed or confused and that you stood with me then and will again, jalapeno peppers, public radio, Richard Hooker, sunsets over Mobile Bay, the tenor solo in Berlioz' *Requiem*, a rising tide of happy memories of my old Kentucky home, West Virginia mountains, Missouri rivers, Alabama beaches, and those who still pray for me there;

And 34 years with the right woman and all the times she's bailed me out, steered me right, given me another chance, and generally put up with me. For these and all your mercies, Lord, your holy Name be praised!

☙ 101.1

I will sing of mercy and justice;
to you, O LORD, will I sing praises.

How can God be both merciful and just? As I see it, if God is just, we're all lost. That's what the Garden of Eden story is about. Adam and Eve are mythical representations of you and me, and their eating of the apple is a picture of our condition before God—guilty. I expect everyone with any moral sensitivity has some vague awareness or memory of what once was, what could have been, or what should be, of the world as God intended it. We are, as Claire Cloninger has said, homesick for Eden, for a world where everyone cares for others and all are provided for, where there are no winners or losers, where sharing and compassion prevail. At the same time, we are also aware of the world as it actually is, a broken, warped, grimy world where everyone is out for himself, some have too much while others have too little, all are losers, and greed prevails. And worst of all, we know that we ourselves are complicit in this world, that we make it what it is. So if God were just, surely he would stamp us out at the first opportunity.

But God is also merciful, so God doesn't do that. Is mercy the mere overlooking of guilt, the way a doting grand-mother fails to see the selfishness of her little darling? I can't think that God overlooks anything, so mercy must be something else. I believe mercy can only occur where the one granting mercy has been wounded. The doting grandmother is not wounded because she doesn't acknowledge the truth. But God *is* truth. God is woundable, vulnerable—*God bleeds*. God takes into himself the suffering that inevitably results from human sin, thereby sparing the guilty party. That's mercy; that's what you see in Jesus.

I don't know how this happens. I've read all the classical theories of the Atonement, and none of them works for me. How the mercy and justice of God relate to each other, I must leave for others to discern. It is a mystery, and gratitude to God is as far into it as I can go.

♋ 102.6-7

I have become like a vulture in the wilderness,
  like an owl among the ruins.
I lie awake and groan;
  I am like a sparrow, lonely on a house-top.

Like the several other laments of individuals found in the Psalter, this psalm contains vivid imagery. Perhaps most striking are these three desolate ornithological images: The psalmist feels like a vulture circling in the sky above the desert, an owl sounding its eerie hoot amidst broken stones and rubble, a sparrow alone on a housetop. There are other telling images as well: The psalmist compares his days to smoke drifting away and a shadow fading as the sun sets (vss. 4, 11), his bones to burning coals (vs. 3), and his heart to withered grass (vs. 4). He forgets to eat (vs. 4), and when he does eat, his food tastes like ashes and his drink like tears (vs. 9).

This kind of language is obviously not meant literally. The power of such writing is in its appeal to the imagination. The reader can *see, feel* and *taste* the psalmist's pain and sense of abandonment. We do not know the specifics of the psalmist's circumstances, and that is perhaps just as well, for it enables us to apply his words to our own circumstances. The psalm also serves as an invitation to the reader who may be experiencing similar feelings to let loose her own imagination so as to devise images of her own. Most people are hit by a devastating experience at some point in their lives—divorce, bereavement, loss of job, illness, addiction, imprisonment, and others. What modern images come to mind to express the feelings such experiences elicit?

It has been many years since I experienced anything so desolating as the psalmist describes, but I recall those times and how just thinking of images that expressed my sense of dereliction and writing them down was some help to me, a kind of prayer. That, I suspect, is also why this psalmist took pen to paper.

❧ 102.23-24

He has brought down my strength before my time;
*   he has shortened the number of my days;*
And I said, "O my God,
do not take me away in the midst of my days...

I have been unusually healthy throughout my 58 years. I know this will not continue forever. I could contract some fatal disease or be struck down in an accident at any moment, even this afternoon, but I don't think about that often. Day to day, I carry on with the perhaps naive assumption that I shall live to a ripe old age. Not knowing firsthand the fears and pains which gave rise to these two verses, I cannot advise the psalmist or anyone else in the prime of life for whom death seems to be knocking at the door. All I can do is imagine the thoughts that might come to me in those circumstances. Among them, I suspect, would be these:

Wait! I'm not finished yet! There are projects I still mean to accomplish, mountains I haven't climbed, broken relationships not yet mended, grandchildren I am yet to hold in my arms, blessings of which I have not taken full advantage. I've put many of these things off until a later time, when I'd have the leisure to tend to them—and this is supposed to be the time! Don't strip me of my good health just yet, Lord.

A gift of 58 healthy years—surely I can give thanks for that when so many others have no healthy years. Deliver me, Lord, from self-pity when I have so much for which to give thanks.

Can I trust you now, Lord? It was easy, or at least easier, to trust you when everything was coming up roses, but now things are coming up thorns, and I find it hard to trust you. I'm scared. What am I scared of? The pain of dying? What lies beyond? Meeting you face to face and having to render an account of myself? All of that, I'm afraid of it all. Please accept me now, Lord, especially my fear. Move me to trust you more deeply and to surrender all things to you, including, my fear, this illness, and my death, and then receive me at the last into your arms.

C₰ 103.2

Bless the LORD, O my soul,
*   and forget not all his benefits.*

Along with Psalm 51, this psalm is read on Ash Wednesday, the most penitential day of the year. Psalm 51 should come as no surprise on that day, replete as it is with references to the burden of sin. It grovels, or comes close to it. But Psalm 103 would seem at first glace an odd choice for Ash Wednesday.

There is hardly a more joyful chapter in the Bible. And yet, Psalm 103 is also about sin, which is presumably why it was chosen for an Ash Wednesday reading. The difference is that in Psalm 51, the author pleads for release from a weight that still burdens him, whereas the author of Psalm 103 seems almost to leap with freedom and joy because the Lord has answered his prayer and lifted the weight from him. Whereas Psalm 51 begs for mercy, Psalm 103 celebrates mercy received, a *fait accompli*, a "done deal."

Psalm 103 begins in an individual vein, with the psalmist addressing his own soul. "Soul," he says, "now you bless the Lord, and don't you forget all he has done for you!" Several hymns ("Praise, my soul, the King of Heaven" and "Praise to the Lord, the Almighty, the King of creation" among them) are based on this psalm, with the singers urging their souls to praise God.

Soon, however, the psalm moves beyond the individual to the whole people of God, as if to say, "Soul, it's not just *your* sin that has been healed and wiped out, but everybody else's, too, so let's *all* join in and bless the Lord!"

Then finally, the psalmist invites the angels, the planets, the galaxies, the heavenly powers, "all you works of his, in all places of his dominion," to join in the song. It seems that sin, brokenness, stain, sickness (all labored over in Psalm 51) affect not just us, but everyone and everything, and that God's salvation extends beyond us into the farthest recesses of his universe. Perhaps Ash Wednesday should be the year's happiest worship service.

↷ 103.11-12

For as the heavens are high above the earth,
    so is his mercy great upon those who fear him.
As far as the east is from the west,
    so far has he removed our sins from us.

Modern cosmology, since the days of Einstein and Planck, has given an entirely new meaning to words like high, above, east, and west. If we thought their meaning elusive before, our minds now are in a new place, where mystery and paradox seem the very definition of reality. Yet passages like this one from Psalm 103 continue to speak to us, perhaps even more tellingly than before. I like to imagine God addressing the sinner newly arrived before his throne in heaven (another of those words):

"Welcome! My door is always open to you. We've been expecting your arrival. I thought you'd probably bring that heavy backpack with you—most people do bring along something of that sort. Now let me have it. That's right, you must turn it over to me. There is no other way. I understand your hesitation. Many people are reluctant to let go of their burden because they've become so attached to it. But doesn't the odor of it bother you? Or have you become inured to the smell of bitterness, self-pity, and vanity? Up here (and never mind where 'up' is), we think what you've brought with you stinks. If you want to remain here, you must relinquish it. That's right—let me have it. And now I'm going to hurl it through the roof, into utmost east and utmost west. Once I have heaved it out of here, it will keep going and going and going, farther and farther from you (and us) so that you couldn't find it again if your life depended on it. Actually, your life *does* depend on your letting go of it, but once it's gone, it's gone for good. I send it into one of my famous black holes, never again to be heard from. Even I couldn't find it again. It shall cease to exist, and I shall not even remember it. I suggest you forget it, too."

℘ 104.25

O LORD, how manifold are your works!
in wisdom you have made them all;
the earth is full of your creatures.

This psalm is unusual in the Bible, almost unique, in that it praises God for the beauties and wonders of nature. Like many people, I feel close to God when I look upon a lovely sunset, enjoy a balmy spring day, take a walk in the woods or along the beach, or sit on my porch listening to the birds as dawn approaches. Part of it is the pleasant sensations—sights, sounds, smells. I suppose that's what people mean when they say they feel closer to God on the golf course than in church. In biblical times, however, nature was seen as a threat and God as the source of protection from it. It was not in nature, but in acts of deliverance, from nature as well as other dangers, that God normally disclosed himself to the Hebrews. God is more than the source of nature for them—God is a Person who creates, sustains, communicates, draws near, retreats, rebukes, chooses, decides, and enjoys a good time. All that suggests we are in *relationship* to God, something nature barely hints at.

The famous hymn gets it exactly right. Yes, we do see God in nature, in the meadows and woodlands "robed in the blooming garb of spring," the sunshine, the moonlight, "and all the twinkling, starry host." The wonders of nature suggest a creative imagination beyond human thinking. But nature only suggests, only hints at God, and a faith based solely on nature can degenerate into a sappy sentimentality that does not challenge, convict, or transform us. That's what "sunset religion" and "golf course religion" tend to be. Our best protection against such a faith is to know and surrender to the One who is God's conclusive act of deliverance: Nature may be fair and pure, but (again in the words of the hymn) "Jesus is fairer, Jesus is purer."

❧ 104.27b

...and there is that Leviathan, which you have made for the sport of it.

Asteroids, storms, centipedes, nettles, flounders, black holes, persimmons, people—why does God make things? Some say God creates because it is the nature of God to create. But that's like saying the sky is blue because it's the nature of the sky to be blue. Others say God creates in order to have someone to love. But that would seem to suggest that God is incomplete or unfulfilled without us to relate to.

I don't know why God creates things. But I like the idea of this psalmist, who looks at one of nature's more implausible creatures, the whale (*leviathan* is the Hebrew word for whale or sea monster), and suggests that God made it simply "for the sport of it." Other translations say God made the whale "as a plaything" or "to amuse" himself. The Bible is full of anthropomorphisms—the attributing of human-like characteristics to God, and most Christians and Jews take this kind of God-language for granted. Play is common not only to human beings, but to animals as well (think of puppy dogs and otters, for example). If the creation mirrors to us something of its Creator, couldn't playfulness be part of the divine nature? Why do so many religious people insist on thinking of God in stern, dour terms?

I like to envision God sitting wherever God sits and dreaming up things that will amuse him: "I think I'll make a funny little wingless bird and plop it down in Antarctica. Then tomorrow, I'll make the Amazon. The day after that, icebergs. Then I'll put together the Crab Nebula, and then grapevines. And then I'll make ocean waves, snowflakes, sunbeams, blueberries, and quarks. Then, for the sport of it, I'll make a huge sea creature that blows air out the top of its head. All this I shall do *just for fun!* Then I'll make human beings and let them wonder why I did it all."

০৪ 105.4

*Search for the L*ORD *and his strength;*
continually seek his face.

Ours is an age of searchers. Time was when no one in the
Western world questioned the reality of God or his place in
God's world (this is still true in most of Africa). But since
about 1700, a new way of thinking has replaced the old in the
West. The same empirical scientific spirit that has brought
us specialized labor, modern medicine, mass communication, world-wide travel, and computers has largely snuffed
out the sense of wonder, mystery, and resignation under
the sovereignty of God that people once felt. This has left a
gaping void in many hearts and souls. We cannot return to
the old ways (though some try to), but we long for something
to fill that void within us. And so we search. Often, we search
in the wrong places—in material consumption, chemicals,
casual sex, status, and power. It may work for a short while,
or seem to work, but we soon feel as empty or emptier than
before. So we continue to search.

What we do not know is that we are not the only
ones searching. God also is searching—*for us.* Of course
God knows where we are, but he is searching for the
moment when we turn to him. The "God" we turn to won't
be the "God" of an earlier era because the human conception of God is ever changing. But the reality designated by
the word "God" remains the same, shrouded in mystery and
power—and in love. It is out of God's love that he seeks us.
John Wesley called this "prevenient grace," God working in
our lives, without our awareness, to bring us to a point where

we open ourselves to him. A modern hymn says it well:

I sought the Lord, and afterward I knew
He moved my soul to seek him, seeking me;
It was not I that found, O Savior true;
No, I was found of thee.

Thou didst reach forth thy hand and mine enfold;
I walked and sank not on the storm-vexed sea;
'Twas not so much that I on thee took hold,
As thou, dear Lord, on me.

I find, I walk, I love, but oh, the whole
Of love is but my answer, Lord, to thee;
For thou were long beforehand with my soul,
Always thou lovest me.

❧ 105.8

He has always been mindful of his covenant,
the promise he made for a thousand
generations.

This psalm is a kind of history lesson. It recounts the major experiences of the Israelite people from the time of Abraham in the 19th century B.C. to the conquest of Canaan in the 13th century B.C. The account includes interpretation, as all history does, for there is no way to tell a story without interpretation. The key thing in the history of Israel as this psalmist (and most biblical authors) sees it is the power and faithfulness of God. God struck a covenant (an agreement that includes a promise) with Abraham, then carried it through, century after century, whether or not Abraham's descendants were faithful to their part of the covenant. What happened doesn't matter as much as the fact that the Israelites saw God's hand in what happened. Events in the political and military arenas weren't just random occurrences, or even the result of human effort, but indications of God at work to bring his promises and purposes to fruition.

This is a way of looking at things that happen in the world. Obviously it is not the only way. Much depends on what you look for. If you expect to see disorder and travesty, that's what you will likely see, but if you look for purpose and direction, that's what you will likely see. Jews and Christians have learned to think as the biblical authors thought—we perceive the hand of God in events taking place in the world today. This is often hard to do. Desmond Tutu speaks of the time when apartheid in South Africa was at its most vicious low point: "We prayed earnestly that God would bless our land and would confound the machinations of the children of darkness. There had been so many moments...when we had preached, 'This is God's world and God is in charge!' Sometimes, when evil seemed to be on the rampage and about to overwhelm goodness, one had held on to this article of faith by the skin of one's teeth. It was a kind of theological whistling in the dark and one was frequently tempted to whisper in God's ear, 'For goodness sake, why don't you make it more obvious that you are in charge?'"

ॐ 106.6

We have sinned as our forebears did;
we have done wrong and dealt wickedly.

Psalm 106 resembles Psalm 105. Both contain recitations of history, with theological interpretation. It has been suggested that the two psalms were used together in liturgical worship. Psalm 106 is the longer of the two and it covers a later period of history, beginning with the exodus from Egypt in the 13th century B.C. and concluding with a reference to the scattering of the people in foreign lands, suggesting a composition in the 6th century B.C. or later. The main difference between the two psalms, however, is their point of view. Whereas Psalm 105 joyously celebrates the Lord's acts of deliverance, Psalm 106 (except for its opening verses) is heavy, mournful, and lugubrious. It tells a sad tale of stupidity and faithlessness by the people of God, acted out again and again. God's acts of deliverance are mentioned, but the focus is on the many times the people turned their backs on God. God appears mainly as a frustrated, justifiably angry figure who seeks, without success, to discipline a people who will not be disciplined.

The psalmist does not tell this tale merely to titillate his readers. He discloses his reason for writing such a psalm in verse 6. What the forebears did of old, the people of today are repeating. The psalm is about ancient history in one sense, but in another, it is about what was happening at the time of writing. Nothing much had changed.

This suggests why we study scripture. It is not to discern doctrines, moral laws, or eternal truths about God (though that can happen, too). We study scripture because we find ourselves in it. The Bible acts like a mirror, showing us who we really are, paring away the self-justifying hypocrisy with which we defend our behaviors, laying bare our true motives and values. It also leads us to see how God acts in the world and in our lives to redeem and transform us. Until the Bible becomes our own story, reading it is of no more value than reading the telephone book. Still, nothing much has changed.

❧ 106.47

Save us, O LORD our God,
and gather us from among the nations,
*   that we may give thanks to your holy Name*
*   and glory in your praise.*

This is the climactic verse of this psalm. It is where the psalmist set out to arrive when he sat down to write this meandering and sad recitation of human perfidy and divine pardoning. "Many a time did he deliver them," he said in verse 43—so now, Lord, *one more time, please!*

We can read the psalm on two levels. First, the psalmist probably had in mind the painful results of the people's faithlessness, including their being driven from their homeland and scattered among foreign nations. He prays that the Lord will gather the people again, bring them home, that they may thank him and glorify him in their own land. God did not intend the story to end in exile and dispersion, and it must not end there. The last chapter must not be a scattering abroad, but a gathering home; not destruction, but restoration.

The psalm can also be read as a plea to God for an inner restoration, a change of heart. In that respect, it is similar to the thought of Jeremiah who, writing at the time of the Babylonian Exile, envisioned a new covenant, not chiseled in stone, but written on the people's hearts (Jer. 31:31-34). If the purpose of the covenant is, in Rowan Williams's words, "a fusion of the faithful promise of God with the faithful obedience of God's people," mere outer restoration will not avail. It is a happy thing if people return to their homes, but if that's all that occurs, nothing important will have occurred. What matters is the relationship. It is as in a marriage. The main thing is not that husband and wife live under the same roof, even that they live comfortably and happily under the same roof. The main thing is their trust of each other and the mutual joy that issues from it.

Book Five

ભ

Psalms 107 through 150

ᏓᎳ 107.4,10, 17,23

...desert wastes....darkness and deep gloom....
rebellious ways....the sea....

What metaphor would come closest to describing the deepest depth to which you have ever sunk? The words "deepest depth" are in fact such a metaphor—you probably knew I was not referring to a distance measurable in feet or meters, but to a condition of the soul. Even today, people speak of feeling "low" or of being "in the depths." Modern idiom offers other images for this condition as well: We say we're in the doldrums (stultifying weather) or have the blues (a cheerless color) or the blahs (senseless talk). Such metaphors can refer to anything from being mildly out of sorts to suicidal despair. When I was at my "deepest depth" some years ago, such images spoke to me. The image that spoke most poignantly to me, though, was of myself as a corpse, lying limp, cold, and colorless in a dark tomb. I could almost feel the smooth stone slab on which my body lay, and the spiders and cockroaches attacking my remains. All the vitality had been drained from me, or so it felt. I was no longer a person, merely a former person.

This psalm consists of four poems, parallel in structure, each based on a different image describing this feeling: The desert is a place without water, haunted by jackals, hyenas, and scorpions. We today still speak of going through "a dry period." We also still describe a sense of hopelessness as "darkness and deep gloom." What the psalmist may have meant by "rebellious ways" we can only guess, but many a rebel has found himself disillusioned later on. And when someone says she is "engulfed" or "drowning" in despair, she uses a biblical metaphor—the sea in the Bible represents untamed chaos. What images from your own experience come to your mind to describe this feeling?

The psalmist has, apparently, "been there." Yet this is hardly a depressing psalm. The psalmist has been there *and back again.* We gain strength in our darker moments by reading the words of someone who has known the darkness but also the light that follows the darkness.

☙ 107.6,8

*Then they cried to the L*ORD *in their trouble,*
and he delivered them from their distress....
*Let them give thanks to the L*ORD *for his mercy*
and the wonders he does for his children.

These two verses represent the heart of this psalm—they are repeated four times. After each of the four images with which the psalmist describes spiritual despair, he repeats these lines, almost as a kind of mantra. This gives the psalm a strong, winsome, upbeat tone.

One of my darker times occurred many years ago when I was captive to a potentially fatal addiction. I had vainly tried for years to control it. Defeated, brokenhearted, and terrified, I finally cried to the Lord in my trouble, and he delivered me from my distress. Why did the Lord do that for me? It wasn't because I had lived a blameless life. Although I could not control my addiction, I had caused it through bad behavioral choices. This psalm mentions four behaviors which led to despair, and each was chosen. Wandering into the desert, sitting down in darkness, rebelling, going off to sea—these were choices; in each case the sufferer had brought this upon himself. But in no case was the Lord's response to rebuke or reject the sufferer. As he did for me, the Lord came to each of them when they cried out to him.

One of the paradoxes of grace (that's the theological word for God's undeserved power and goodness in people's lives) is that while it arises solely from the loving heart of God, is freely given, and in no way depends on our merits, yet in many cases (perhaps not all, but certainly in my own) a willingness or readiness to receive God's grace seems to be a prerequisite. It is as if the Lord waits patiently (or perhaps not so patiently?) for an invitation to come to our rescue. So what caused me to turn finally to God in my addiction after years of refusing to do so? I don't know—but I suspect God had something to do even with that decision on my part.

ଔ 107.33,35

The LORD changed rivers into deserts,
and water-springs into thirsty ground...
He changed deserts into pools of water
and dry land into water-springs.

Paradox, again. It's throughout the Bible, but rarely does it slap you in the face as it does here. Is God on the side of the wets or the drys in these lines, or is he on both sides, or on neither side, or does he switch sides? I feel like saying, "Lord, if you want us to walk in your ways, at least be consistent about where you walk! When you keep switching paths, how can you expect us to stay on the right path?" I don't know how the Lord would respond to such words, but it wouldn't surprise me if he said, "I have purposes of which you know nothing, and even if you did know something of them, you wouldn't understand them. But you only have to take one step at a time. If you're serious about staying on the right path, the next step is usually pretty clear to you, or it should be, and if it isn't, then you haven't been honest with yourself." To which I would probably respond, "Yes, Sir, I'm sorry I asked."

Those who can't live with paradox have a tough time with the God of the Bible. One way to deal with that, of course, is to distort the God of the Bible, to change paradox to platitude, mystery to monotony, spirit to flesh. We do it all the time because it's easier that way and we can be in control. But there's no truth in it. The truth is, as St. Paul says, that we see "through a glass darkly." That we fail to perceive plan and purpose does not mean there is no plan or purpose. It says nothing about God or God's reality, but it says a lot about our paltry range of vision. Faith is always a risk, an act of trust, a stepping out into the fog. The alternative to faith is staying put, but there is no security in that. If we sit comfortably with our easy truths, pretending to know what we cannot know, our souls die of self-satisfied atrophy.

ॐ 108

When preparing for the publication of my book *Glorious Companions: Five Centuries of Anglican Spirituality*, I learned a few things about copyright laws. The book was to have had a chapter on each of 30 Anglican spiritual writers, but it ended up with just 29 chapters because the estate of one recently deceased author refused to grant permission to quote from his works unless I paid an exorbitant fee. Had I gone ahead and printed the author's words without permission, my publisher and I could have been hauled into court and slapped with a hefty fine.

There were no copyright laws in biblical times, nor had the word plagiarism been invented. You wouldn't have been sued or even frowned upon for using other people's material without paying a fee and citing your source. In fact, biblical authors frequently borrowed from each other's work and that of other writers. It was done all the time, and no one gave it a thought. If you heard something you liked, you claimed it and passed it on. No one cared where it had come from or who had written it. This psalm is perhaps the Bible's foremost example of that sort of borrowing—hardly a word of it is original. The first half comes, practically word for word, from Psalm 57, and the second half from Psalm 60. Or perhaps this psalmist lifted from the same now lost sources that the other two psalmists used. In any case, our psalmist didn't bother to cite his sources.

Things I've written have sometimes shown up in other publications, usually but not always attributed to me. I've never cared when people reprinted my material. In fact, I've been flattered. But now that I've begun writing and publishing entire books rather than just short articles, I suppose I'd be miffed if someone lifted whole paragraphs from me and didn't mention where they'd come from—and I'd appreciate a small check, or at least a thank-you note. On the whole, though, I like the unassuming freedom in these matters with which the ancients operated. Pride of authorship was apparently unknown in those days, and the subject matter—God, in this case—was more important than the identity of the person writing about it.

ᏍᎬ 109.3-4

Despite my love, they accuse me;
  but as for me, I pray for them.
They repay evil for good,
  and hatred for my love.

Presumably, this psalmist expected to be taken seriously. But the psalm is so savagely vicious and self-righteous that it almost makes me smile—the psalmist's anger is so out of control that it approaches a comic caricature. But it was apparently real, and therefore dangerous. The psalmist is consumed by vengeance, praying not merely to get even, but that God inflict ghastly tortures upon those who have wronged him and upon their families. He says that he prays for them, but if the rest of the psalm is an indication, he actually prays against them. This is one man to whom I would say, "Please *don't* remember me in your prayers."

What was done to this psalmist? The psalm gives no details. Some unidentified persons, it seems, have lied to him, cursed him, and accused him of wrongdoing. Or perhaps the psalmist has, in his obsession with himself and his own virtue, concocted a list of imaginary slights. Either way, he has left no room in his soul for humility, penitence, forgiveness, or reconciliation. He has left no room in his soul for God.

How did psalms of this sort (this isn't the only one) get into the Bible? I don't know. They have been an embarrassment to more than one sensitive reader. The only use I can imagine for them is to hold them up before me as a kind of mirror when similar sentiments invade my own soul. Let us not allow what disgusts us in this psalmist to disgust others should they overhear our prayers.

☙ 109.5-19

Set a wicked man against him....Let his days be few....Let his children be fatherless....Let the creditor seize everything he has....Let there be no one to show him kindness....

Goodness me! I'd say you've got some issues! You need to get a handle on your anger, fellow. No, don't tell me what he did to you. I don't need to know what it was. That's not the problem, not now, anyway. Or at least it's not a problem you can do anything about. What's done is done, however unfair and awful it may have been. You can't undo it. But I don't blame you for being angry. When crimes and injustices are committed against people, anger is understandable, maybe even natural, and I think it's okay. But don't water and fertilize it; don't let it grow. Let your anger run its course, then fade away.

And for heaven's sake don't act on your anger. The way you're talking now, it wouldn't surprise me if you decided to make those thoughts of yours come true. You wouldn't actually do something to make his children fatherless, would you? Nor would it surprise me if you did something to yourself. People consumed with anger and self-pity—and pardon me, but I think that's what we've got here—sometimes do violence to themselves. It's okay to be angry, but you can't hold on to that anger forever without alienating everyone around you and eventually destroying yourself.

I'm glad you're writing stuff like this. Writing it down is a good way to vent your anger. I've done that when I've been in a rage at someone who had slighted or hurt me. It gets it out from within you. When you put it onto the paper, it is not inside you any longer, so keep writing until it's all out of you. That's what needs to happen. If your rage stays inside you, it will devour you like a ravenous lion. So go ahead and get it on paper. Entertain every vile, foul, cruel thought that comes into your mind. Visualize it. Write it down. Then let it go.

↶ 110.1

The LORD said to my Lord, "Sit at my right hand, until I make your enemies your footstool."

New Testament authors make much of this psalm. They quote or refer to it 19 times, more than any other chapter in the

Hebrew scriptures. Most of the New Testament references to Psalm 110 are to this verse, and for the modern reader unfamiliar with Hebrew, it raises a perplexing question having to do with the word *lord*. In most English translations, the Hebrew name for God, represented in Hebrew by the letters YHWH and probably pronounced "Yahweh," is rendered as "the LORD," usually in small capital letters. At other times, the word lord refers to a human ruler, as in medieval Europe. Both usages occur here. A less ambiguous translation might be "Yahweh said to my king..." Originally, the psalm referred to David or some other king of Israel, but New Testament authors see in the verse a reference to God the Father raising Jesus the Son to sit at his right hand in heaven.

This is an example of anthropomorphism, using human concepts, such as a feudal lord, to refer to God. The Bible is full of this; Jews and Christians use such language routinely. But Muslims regard anthropomorphism as demeaning to God, who is far above anything human, and a human-like God would be inconceivable to a Buddhist.

I am unabashedly anthropomorphic in addressing God in prayer. Of course I realize God can be envisioned in human terms only in an analogous way—God is not *literally* a feudal lord, a shepherd, a judge, a father or mother, or whatever. Much harm is done when such language is taken literally. The Muslims are right in that God is far more than anything human language can say about him. Yet human language, limited as it is, is the only language we have, and some human words can point to God. If we had nothing in common with God at all, we could never relate to God. In a mysterious way far beyond our probing, God is *like* a lord, a shepherd, a judge. And for Christians, the ultimate anthropomorphism was an act on the part of God himself—his taking on human flesh in the person of Jesus Christ.

∞ 110.4b

"You are a priest for ever after the order of Melchizedek."

Melchizedek is a shadowy figure who appears just once in the Bible, in Genesis 14:18, seemingly out of nowhere. He is there identified as "king of Salem" (Salem is a shortened form of Jerusalem) and "priest of God Most High." Melchizedek is referred to in two other places in the Bible, in this psalm, where he is a prototype for a king in the Davidic line (later taken to mean the long awaited Messiah), and in the New Testament Epistle to the Hebrews, where he is a figure for Christ. His significance, both for the psalmist and for the author of Hebrews, seems to be that he combines two usually separate roles, those of king and priest.

These two later uses of the figure of Melchizedek illustrate one way that religious ideas and symbols work. Communities of faith have long histories, sometimes encompassing thousands of years. Over time, they build traditions consisting of many branches and layers. As times change, perspectives and priorities evolve. A new generation of believers often discovers something in its tradition that had been marginal or forgotten before, but which in a later time takes on fresh significance, perhaps quite different from its original import.

The entire community sometimes discovers new meaning in old symbols, or an individual, meditating upon the tradition, can do it. Many of the meditations in this book are examples of this. As I prayed through the Psalter and a particular image or idea lodged in my mind, I tried to give it free rein, following it wherever it chose to go. Sometimes it triggered a distant personal memory and provided new insight into its meaning. At other times it provided a new vantage point from which to look at a familiar theological idea, or revealed connections between seemingly unrelated things that I had not noted before. I never knew where it would lead me, but I have found that using the scriptures (and other elements of Christian tradition) in this way, infuses my prayers with energy—new meanings from old images.

⚛ 111.1a

Hallelujah!

This is the first of seven psalms in a row beginning or ending with this acclamation. It also concludes (and usually introduces as well) Psalms 104 to 106 and 146-150. Though the derivation of *hallelujah* is uncertain, it is probably formed from *hallel*, praise, and *jah*, a shortened form of the divine name. It means, "Praise the Lord!"

Hallelujah was a liturgical expression in ancient Israel, but like the English "praise the Lord," it may have been spoken outside liturgical settings as well. We use that expression, in either its Hebrew or its English form, when we receive good news—our cake does not fall, we pass an exam, the IRS decides not to audit our tax returns, our biopsy comes back negative, a truce is signed in a long-running conflict.

But how does one actually praise the Lord? By shouting it out at praise meetings, certainly. By singing hymns, certainly. But words are cheap. As with the words "I love you," if "Praise the Lord" merely expresses a feeling of coziness with God, it doesn't mean much. Commitment and action put flesh on words such as these. Do we *do* what we say? I squirm when I imagine how God might respond to the "Praise the Lord!" that often passes my lips:

"What do you mean when you say that, Dick? I notice you say it a lot. You like to hang around churches and you sing the hymns so loud that people sometimes stare at you. You also pray to me and praise my name every day in private. And sometimes you just say 'Praise the Lord!' for no apparent reason. Okay, fine. That does you no harm, I suppose—at least there are some sins you can't wallow in while praying (but some are more tempting when you pray, so be careful). Anyway, I've heard your 'Praise the Lord!' thousands of times, and I don't need to keep hearing it. Frankly, I'm tired of hearing it—I'd like to see it. All these hallelujahs—what change do they effect in your life?"

৫ 111.10a

The fear of the Lord is the beginning of wisdom.

I cringe when I recall the remark I made to a distinguished and devout Old Testament scholar on the faculty of Vanderbilt Divinity School when I began studies there in 1967. I had no intention of becoming a priest in those days—my goal was to acquire an advanced academic degree in the scriptures, then teach in a college or university. Academics had always appealed to me and my intellectual faculties had been well honed by 1967. I related to God (as I related to everything in those days) as a concept, but I shied away from talking about personal faith. I told the professor that I intended to study the Bible and teach it to students but that religious devotion and commitment would not be part of it for me. He gave me a stunned look and said, "Then you won't learn anything that matters from your study of the Bible."

The professor was right, of course, and as he probably suspected even then, more was going on within me than I knew—otherwise, why would I be choosing to study the Bible, which is all about God, rather than, say, chemistry or economics? I was perplexed, smug, and defensive where personal faith was concerned, but passion for God lay not far beneath my smooth academic veneer. I was hungering for God, whether I acknowledged it or not, and I was soon drawn into a conscious, intentional commitment that I hadn't anticipated.

Wisdom begins when we are in right relationship to God. One can be smart but not wise, or wise but uneducated. Academic pursuits still draw me (I teach in a seminary these days) and I still enjoy debating theological conundrums. Intellectually, I still question everything, from the existence of God to the smallest doctrinal point. But I no longer relate to God as a concept. I wrestle with God, play with God, weep with God, argue with God, laugh with God, love God—and fear God, as a power I cannot manipulate or control. I find God—or perhaps I should say God finds me—not in my mind, but in my heart—or maybe it's in my gut.

ca 112.1b

Happy are they who fear the Lord
and have great delight in his commandments!

And what commandments would these be? There are the famous ten, of course, found in Exodus 20 and Deuteronomy 5, and the psalmist may have had them in mind. Most people today couldn't recite the Ten Commandments, but they've heard of them. Then there are the many specific commandments found in the first five books of the Hebrew scriptures (several hundred were identified by later rabbis). And for Christians, there are the various words of Jesus that sound like commandments: "Do not look dismal....Ask, and it will be given to you....Come unto me....Love one another as I have loved you....Do this in remembrance of me."

One of the Prayer Book collects asks God to "make us love what you command," which is almost a paraphrase of the line from the psalm about taking "great delight" in God's commandments. Most people don't think of commandments in terms of love and delight. That's because we think of them as imposed from outside by some external authority such as a sheriff, a school principal, or a parent, whom we often resent. We want to be free to do our own thing, to stretch our wings and fly where we choose. Authorities that restrain us are not loved. But God is not such an authority. God grants us the freedom to do exactly as we choose, and we have plunged off in all directions, with often woeful consequences. God's commandments are summed up in one short sentence, and it is an option, not an order—*Love God and our neighbor.* The consequences of disobedience are not imposed upon us like a penalty, but arise out of the nature of the commandment itself: Only those who give love are able to receive it. Some people receive love first, having never previously known it, which moves them to give it in return. But those who repeatedly turn their backs so they do not have to embrace God and other people also close off the possibility of being embraced. To love or delight in what God commands is to receive the love of God and to love God in return.

℃ 113.5

Who is like the LORD our God, who sits enthroned on high,
but stoops to behold the heavens and the earth?

Imagine a conversation between God and one of his angels about two thousand years ago:

"I'm about ready to give up on the whole project. I've tried nearly everything—miraculous deliverances, carving do's and don'ts into stone tablets, military victories, military defeats, visions in the middle of the night. Nothing fazes them. It's as if I weren't there. But then, I'm not actually *there*—and I've begun to think maybe that's the problem. Do you suppose it would make a difference if I went down there in person?

"*You mean become one of them? Are you crazy, Lord? Why would you want to do that? Have you forgotten who you are? You are the Lord God Almighty, Creator of the universe. Your place is here, Lord, enthroned on high, where we can sing to you, bow to you, and adore you. Don't you love hearing that* 'Sanctus! Sanctus! Sanctus!' *echoing across the glassy sea all day and all night—of course you love it, and you're entitled to it. Claim it! You have no idea what might happen to you if you went down there and got mixed up with those creatures."*

"Actually, I do have some idea. I've been thinking about it for a long time. I figure they'd probably turn on me and kill me. You say that being immortal and all, I can't be killed? Well, you just watch. I'm God, so I can agree to be killed if I want to. If I went down there in person and met them face to face, not in all my heavenly majesty, but in weakness and humility, and if I endured the worst they could throw at me, maybe then they'd know I love them and want them to come home to me. Anyway, I've tried everything else, and this is a last resort, but I think it might just work. No objections, now—I've made up my mind. Notify the heavenly host to start practicing a suitable anthem, and tell them no more *sanctus*—I'm weary of that. Something new, please. And tell them they'll have nine months to rehearse."

℞ 114.2-4

Judah became God's sanctuary
and Israel his dominion.
The sea beheld it and fled;
Jordan turned and went back.
The mountains skipped like rams,
and the little hills like young sheep.

We tend to think in terms of opposites: Spirit and flesh, light and darkness, for or against, true or false, living or inanimate—one or the other, not both, and nothing halfway in between. The Bible is full of that sort of thing, so our seeing things in terms of opposites must point to something fundamental in the universe as God has set it up. But occasionally we find in the scriptures suggestions of a different way of understanding things. These verses make such a suggestion, and there may be truth in what they suggest.

Rather than always think in terms of opposites, would we do better sometimes to envision creation in terms of a spectrum? At one end of the spectrum is pure spirit—angels and other heavenly beings. At the other end is pure matter—rocks from outer space. Most things, however, lie somewhere between, partaking in varying degrees of both spirit and matter. This would include those peculiar hybrids of spirit and matter, human beings, as well as living habitats such as seas, rivers, mountains, hills—and our planet itself.

This psalm celebrates God's rescuing of his people from slavery and his presence within and among them, and it envisions all creation responding, each creature using the voice God has given to it. Fanciful as the language may be, could there be some truth in the vision of the sea bolting off, rivers turning around and running the other way, and mountains and hills skipping for joy, all in response to what they see that God is doing?

℘ 115.1

Not to us, O LORD, not to us,
but to your Name give glory;
  because of your love and because of your
   faithfulness.

We like to be appreciated for things we do—tasks completed, children reared, goals achieved, home runs hit. There is nothing wrong in this. Pleasure in accomplishment is a good and natural thing. The problem arises when we claim title to something because of what we assume are our superior abilities. This is a form of idolatry, valuing of self (expressed by grasping for something we want) more than we value God. This psalm disavows idolatry, almost to the point of ridicule or sarcasm. The psalmist says we glory in worthless, inert objects, and that those who do so aren't much better than the objects themselves.

  Think of the things which modern people value but which amount to nothing in the end: Physical beauty—most of our features were determined at birth by genetics, and even if we enhance our looks by diet and exercise, the capacity to do so is a gift from God. Social connections—even if some people were the "right kind of people" (a dubious assumption), all people come from God and return to God, where such distinctions evaporate. Wealth—the one who really owns it is the one from whom it comes and to whom it shall return in the end. Books published, CD's cut, paintings painted, music composed—while we rightly enjoy creative activities, our creativity comes from God. Power—individuals and nations crave power over others, but ultimately all power resides in God and he will have the final say.

So why do we waste time glorying in what amounts to nothing and passes so quickly from us? Where do such delusions come from and what makes us cling to them? And what stops us even now from putting them behind us and embracing the truth?

✑ 115.16

The heaven of heavens is the LORD's,
  but he entrusted the earth to its peoples.

I don't like the word stewardship because it has largely lost its meaning. To most church people, it suggests fundraising. I prefer the word trusteeship because in today's language it means what stewardship once meant. A trustee is someone entrusted with the responsibility of managing the assets of another. Parents are often designated trustees of their children's assets; banks are trustees for persons unable to manage their own affairs. A trustee is not the owner, but is accountable to the owner, charged with managing the owner's assets on behalf of the owner and according to the owner's purposes and designs.

Everything under the heavens is God's because he makes it. But God entrusts the earth to human beings, names us trustees over this small portion of his estate. When we speak of "our" money, "our" family, "our" land, "our" time, it is a polite fiction, a mere figure of speech. Nothing is ours—all is God's, but God allows us to manage what is his, to do with it as we wish, for a brief time. This doesn't mean we must never buy anything we want, for God has filled his world with delights for our happiness. Accumulating beyond our need, however, is not part of the divine plan. John Wesley had it right: "Gain all you can, without hurting either yourself or your neighbor...Save all you can, by cutting off every expense which serves only to indulge foolish desire...And then give all you can, or in other words, give all you have to God.... Render to God not a tenth, not a third, not a half, but all that is God's, be it more or less, by employing all on yourself, your household, the household of faith, and all mankind, in such a manner that you may give a good account of your stewardship when ye can be no longer stewards..."

When we die, our trusteeship will pass to another. What will we say when we are asked to render an account of our management of God's earth?

ॐ 116.2-3

The cords of death entangled me;
the grip of the grave took hold of me;
I came to grief and sorrow.
Then I called upon the Name of the LORD:
"O LORD, I pray you, save my life."

Lazarus lay in the tomb for four days, by which time he had begun to stink. I lay in my tomb for several years, and I suspect a foul odor had begun to emanate from my soul.

I did not know I was entering a tomb when I made a series of important decisions, that I convinced myself were the right decisions but the motivation for which was, in large part, to gratify my ego. At first I felt vibrant and proud of what I had achieved. But in time, I found myself increasingly alone, frightened, tense, and angry. Finally, I realized that although my lungs continued to breathe and my heart continued to beat, my soul had died. I was shriveled and immobilized, no longer able even to do the things I once had done easily and well. I wanted to run away, but had no place to run to. The "cords of death" seemed to have wrapped themselves around my soul. I felt trapped and that I was sinking into quicksand.

I called upon the Lord to save me. It was a desperate plea directed into what I felt certain were empty heavens, to a God I suspected I had merely imagined. I no longer really believed in God, though I continued to work in his church, mostly because that was the work I knew how to do and I lacked energy to seek out anything else. I called out to God from habit more than from expectation, and because I had no one else to call to.

Then, in ways I couldn't have expected, God picked me up, fluffed me like a sat-on pillow, refreshed me, taught me to laugh and dance again, and started me on a new and happy road. Could I have been raised to the life I enjoy today if I had not first died?

ca 116.10,13

How shall I repay the LORD
for all the good things he has done for me?....
Precious in the sight of the LORD
is the death of his servants.

God has been good to me, and I know it. But why does counting my blessings so often make me feel more guilty than joyful?

I think it is that I have not yet heard, or not yet fully believed, that God loves me. I still carry with me an old notion that my relationship to God is like that of an employee to an employer, in which God "pays" me with blessings in exchange for some "service" I render to him, and if I fail to carry through my part of the deal, I run the risk of being terminated. I have a vision in my head of God coming to me some day, handing me my pink slip, and saying, "Your services are no longer needed. Clean out your desk and get out of here." Besides, even if our relationship to God were of this sort, how could we possibly repay the One who gives us life itself and everyone and everything that comes with it? It's a laughable thought. Why even try?

Where this old misunderstanding of how God relates to us came from, I don't know. It did not come from God. God has made clear that he wants to be our loving parent, not our boss, and as a parent myself, I should understand what this means. When I do something for my own children, I want not to be paid back, but to be loved and trusted. When my children were infants, I delighted in holding them in my arms, while they did nothing but sleep peacefully, contentedly, trustingly. I wanted to give my love, not be paid for it. God is like that, too, only more so.

Perhaps that is why the death of his servants is precious in God's sight. Death, for those who fully understand and accept that God loves them, is the ultimate act of trust.

൦ 117

Praise the LORD, all you nations;
laud him, all you peoples.
For his loving-kindness toward us is great,
and the faithfulness of the LORD endures
for ever.
Hallelujah!

The shortest chapter in the Bible at a mere 17 words in Hebrew, this psalm is printed above in its entirety. Despite its brevity, the psalm is comprehensive in scope, bidding all nationalities and peoples to praise the Lord. No narrow ethnic exclusivism here. What would have to happen for this bidding to become a reality?

I read the Bible daily and praise God for his goodness to me. Of course, I do—who wouldn't feel contented in my circumstances? I am in good health, happily married, have pleasant work to do, and live in a comfortable home where my needs are well provided for. It is easy for me to envision a loving God. But how does a Palestinian whose home has been taken from him feel about the loving-kindness of God? How does an Israeli whose loved one was murdered in a suicide bombing feel about the loving-kindness of God? How does someone living with AIDS whose family and friends have disowned him feel about it? How does a child in the Sudan who has been kidnaped and forced into slave labor feel about it, or a parent whose child has been killed in a traffic accident, or a woman whose husband has beaten or abandoned her?

Yes, let all the nations, all the peoples praise the Lord. By all means. But I do not look for this to happen until there is a change in those of us who now praise the Lord—perhaps easily, perhaps routinely, perhaps without pausing to ask who the Lord is or what it means to praise him. All peoples will praise the Lord for his loving-kindness when the loving-kindness of those who claim the Lord's name is as limitless as the loving-kindness of the Lord himself. Until that happens, why should others praise this God of ours?

෨ 118.17

I shall not die, but live,
and declare the works of the LORD.

Some years ago, the rector of a neighboring parish battled valiantly against lung cancer for over two years. His witness to the power of God inspired his congregation and others who knew him. I am one of many who prayed for him daily. This psalm, and this verse in particular, sustained him and his wife through their ordeal.

In one sense, of course, the first line of this verse is just not true—every one of us will die. Death raises troubling questions for us, especially the death of someone we love, someone who dies at a young age, or someone who suffers greatly while dying. But death itself is a natural, normal thing. Death is not the opposite of life, but part of life created and ordained by God. God set up the world this way, and there are good reasons for it. The question is *how* we will die, and I don't mean by what means or in what circumstances, but what significance our death will have for us and those near us. I have seen people die amidst intense, prolonged pain, but whose departure from this life blessed and inspired family, friends, health professionals, and all who knew them. I have seen others die who burdened and abused those around them by their cynicism, anger, and clutching for control. The difference was that those who blessed and inspired others had learned to surrender command, to turn over both body and spirit to God—they had learned to trust. The others insisted on being in charge and having things their way.

St. Francis greeted death as his sister because he had learned to entrust all things to God. When I lie dying, I hope I can be still, let go, and let God be God, welcoming my death as yet another gift from the hand of a tender and winsome Lord. If I can do that, I shall declare the works of the Lord, both in my life and in my death.

ᛜ 118.24

On this day the LORD has acted;
we will rejoice and be glad in it.

When I rise in the morning, I thank God for the gift of another day. Then I pray through the day as I envision it: Whom shall I see? What shall I read or write? Where shall I go? To whom shall I speak? Who has asked me to pray for them today? Since the day rarely unfolds exactly as I envision it upon rising, I also pray for the unforeseen event. As God gave the day to me, I give it back to God. Often I sing some hymn of dedication, such as "Take my life and let it be" or "Awake, my soul, and with the sun."

The important thing is to focus on *today*. This does not mean we are to give no thought to yesterday or tomorrow, for today's tasks include honoring yesterday's commitments and planning for tomorrow. But we live in the present moment. We cannot respond to God yesterday or tomorrow—we can only respond to God today. In his book *Abandonment to Divine Providence*, Jean Pierre de Caussade writes: "To be satisfied with the present moment is to relish and adore the divine will moving through all we have to do and suffer as events crowd in upon us....The present moment is always overflowing with immeasurable riches, far more than you are able to hold....Our only satisfaction must be to live in the present moment as if there were nothing to expect beyond it."

Obsessing about yesterday and tomorrow is a constant temptation. When I have spoken out of line or embarrassed myself yesterday, my mind wants to brood over it. When tomorrow is likely to include a tough test or confrontation, my mind wants to worry about it. Living in the present moment excludes brooding, but often affords an opportunity to make amends for yesterday and to pray and prepare for tomorrow's challenge. *Today* is the day the Lord acts; we are to rejoice and be glad in *today*.

ॐ 119.1

Happy are they whose way is blameless,
who walk in the law of the LORD!

Some people regard this psalm as a tedious, artificially contrived poem from a rigid, legalistic, little mind. The Bible's longest chapter at 176 verses, it is an acrostic poem, consisting of 22 strophes of eight verses each, with one strophe for each letter of the Hebrew alphabet. Each of the first eight verses begins with the letter *aleph*, the first letter in the alphabet. Then come eight verses beginning with *beth*, the second letter, and so on through *taw*, the 22nd and final letter. It is an extraordinarily confining way to write a poem, like writing a song in which the first eight measures begin with A, the second eight with B flat, and so on. Moreover, all but five verses contain a reference to the commandments, judgments, decrees, words, promises, or statutes of God, which in this psalm mean close to the same thing and to which the psalmist swears his loyalty again and again and again and again. Were it not for the acrostic structure of the psalm, its 176 verses could probably have been put in any order—there is no apparent movement of thought within the psalm. More than one reader has found it monotonous.

But there is another way to look at Psalm 119. What sort of person would write something like this? Not a scatterbrained, on-again-off-again, spur-of-the-moment free spirit, I'd say, but someone who loves order and structure and perhaps has little of it in his life. The psalmist does give us hints of his circumstances—he is "deeply troubled" (vs. 107) and indignant (vs. 139) because of enemies who taunt him (vs. 42) and set a trap for him (vs. 110). But rather than curse them, this psalmist pens an elaborate hymn praising the ways of God as revealed in his commandments. He commits himself to what he knows to be right and promises to meditate on it day and night. We should not think of the psalm as legalistic, for its spirit is one of commitment to the will of God, not criticism of those who fall short of it. Tedious as some may find it, others find in this psalm a sublime hymn of submission to the divine will.

❧ 119.32

I will run the way of your commandments,
for you have set my heart at liberty.

The pelican flaps his wings and then glides motionless, inches above the surface of the bay. Then he flaps his wings and glides some more. Occasionally, when he feels like it, he rises a few feet into the air until he spots a fish near the surface of the water. Then he plops into the bay for his breakfast. Then he finds a piling beyond the pier where he takes a nap.

I am sure the pelican is content with his pelicanhood. He flaps, glides, rises, plops, eats, and naps. Then he does it all over again. He is not angry or grieved or anxious because he cannot climb an oak tree or burrow into the ground. The pelican is at liberty because he does as a pelican is meant to do and is content to do it.

We are not free like the pelican. God created us to serve and enjoy him and has given his commandments to guide the way. But we have other ideas; we are not content to be who God created us to be and do what God enables us to do. At times we want to be an animal or a bird, perhaps even a pelican. If only we could flap and glide and rise as the pelican does, we'd be content, we tell ourselves. At other times we would be some other person, someone wealthier, more famous, more handsome, or more influential. We tell ourselves we'd be happy if only we could be what other people are and do what other people do. At other times, we want to be an angel or spirit, to gaze upon the face of God untroubled by insoluble mysteries. We tell ourselves we'd be happy if only we could see what we cannot see and know what we cannot know.

The chains that bind us from claiming that abundant life which God has made known in Jesus are inside our souls and are self-imposed. We choose captivity over freedom. True liberty is obedience to God. Free us from our chains, O God, for although we have bound ourselves in them, we cannot free ourselves from them. Set us free to run the way of your commandments.

℘ 119.33-37

Teach me...Give me...Make me...Incline my heart...Turn my eyes.

Many people feel guilty, unaccepted and unacceptable, and the drive to win God's favor is a primary motivating force in their lives. They see life as a test administered by God. If they make a passing score, they go to heaven; if they flunk; they go to hell. Not only is this a dreary way to see life, but it's a sure route to failure and disillusionment because all our devices to pass the test, to win God's favor, are futile. God's standards are absolute and unnegotiable—God does not grade on the curve. We can do many things by virtue of our hard work, intelligence, personality, and piety, but these things will all fall short of the mark. They will not please God. We don't have what it takes to please God.

But God has what it takes to please God. We do not free ourselves from guilt by trying harder to please God—rather, God frees us. It is not what we do, but what we allow God to do in us. The verbs in these verses tell the tale. They focus not on what the psalmist will do, but on what he asks God to do within him. God teaches, gives, creates. God bends the psalmist's heart, turns the psalmist's eyes. The psalmist's role is to invite God in, then to submit and obey. If we must think in terms of passing a test, God *gives* a score of 100 percent to any who ask for it. This doesn't mean, of course, that we immediately cease to be sinners. Rather, God's grace works in us and among us gradually, transforming us moment to moment, like yeast rising or the day growing warmer as the sun ascends into the sky.

In the paradoxical words of the 19th century hymn writer George Matheson:

> *Make me a captive, Lord, and then I shall be free.*
> *Force me to render up my sword, and I shall conqueror be.*
> *I only stand unbent amid the clashing strife,*
> *When on thy bosom I have leant, and found in*
> *Thee my life.*

❧ 120.5

How hateful it is that I must lodge in Meshech and dwell among the tents of Kedar!

This is the first of a collection of psalms (120 through 134) known as the Songs of Ascents, to be sung by pilgrims on their way to Jerusalem. Meshech is in Asia Minor and Kedar in Arabia. Both are far from Jerusalem, and they are far from each other. The psalmist could not have lived in both places and may in fact never have lived in either. He may have chosen these two remote localities to represent all strange, alien places. The psalmist almost certainly did live far from his homeland, however, and like many who reside among people of a different language, culture, and religion, he distrusted his neighbors, suspecting them of talking against him and of plotting war. He found living among them "hateful."

"Alienation" became a popular concept in the 20th century. Many people, including some who had never left the place of their birth, experienced their world as an alien environment. I felt that way twice, as an adolescent, and again 25 years later. I thought no one shared my feelings, interests, and hopes. It was as if I spoke a language different from everyone else. As an adolescent, I spoke the language of classical music, English literature, and baseball, while everyone else (at least it seemed like everyone else) spoke the language of rock and roll, movies, and football. I thought I was an oddity and would never have friends or family. Later, my sense of alienation arose from a difference in values and dreams between me and those with whom I associated day to day. I felt disconnected, a stranger in my own land.

I've learned that the way to deal with the sense of alienation isn't to lament that we live in Meshech or Kedar, but to look around us for potential colleagues among whom we can grow to become the persons God intends us to be. Every place is an alien land if we allow it to be. And perhaps we ourselves could be the needed comrade in another person's Meshech or Kedar.

♋ 121.1

I lift up my eyes to the hills;
from where is my help to come?

I shall never read or hear this psalm without thinking of Bald Knob overlooking the Reems Creek valley in Buncombe County, North Carolina. As a boy, I spent several weeks each summer at a camp in the Reems Creek Valley. On Sunday mornings, we would walk to a spot called Inspiration Point (what else?), for worship. We often recited this psalm. Seated on our wooden benches at Inspiration Point, we looked up at Bald Knob, which seemed to return our gaze from far across the valley. For years, I thought the second part of this verse was not a question, but a statement (as the King James Version does in fact seem to suggest): "I will lift up mine eyes unto the hills, from whence cometh my help." I knew better than to take those words literally—the mountain was just a big pile of dirt and rock, after all, not likely to help a small boy. But Bald Knob was for me a symbol for the rock-like reliability of God. The psalm made me feel secure.

I still treasure this psalm for the assurances of divine care which it suggests. But when I consider that this was a pilgrim psalm and ask what this verse might have meant to ancient travelers, I get a different nuance. Presumably, the hills referred to are not those of Jerusalem, for the traveling pilgrims had not yet reached their destination. These were other hills, strange hills alongside an unfamiliar road far from home. They could be sheltering wild animals, or robbers who would know quite well the times of year when pilgrims would be passing through the valley below. Read this way, the question in the second part of the verse becomes a real one, born of danger—*Where can I find help?* The rest of the psalm then serves to assure the worried pilgrim that day and night, his God does not sleep and will protect his beloved from all evil.

Unhappy things do, of course, happen to people who trust God. The psalm's meaning is not so simple as that. I take it as an assurance that even when unhappy things happen, even in the midst of them, God is there to hold us up, strengthen us, and receive us at the last.

❧ 121.4

Behold, he who keeps watch over Israel
shall neither slumber nor sleep.

On the whole, I like this thought. There are, of course, some things about myself, a few thoughts and fantasies at the very least, which I'd just as soon God not know about. Should he happen to doze off when I entertain those thoughts and fantasies, that would suit me fine. But most of the time, I like thinking of God as perpetually awake.

It suggests to me that even when I'm asleep, or when I'm awake to the world but asleep to God, that God is still on duty running the world, or at least paying attention to it. I can't believe that God intends or plans everything that happens, but I like knowing that he's aware of it.

That God sees everything further suggests that God, because he is also almighty, will see that justice is done in the end. The whole justice thing is a murky mystery to me.

If I were in charge, justice (or at least justice as I envision it) would be done—and sooner, and more decisively. This is, clearly, not God's way, for reasons known only to God. But God is always awake, always taking note, overlooking nothing, and that seems to say that in God's own way, obscure as that may at times seem to me, he will see that things end up right. They seem far from right just now, so I like the thought that the world won't always be like this.

Finally, in a more personal vein, if God neither slumbers nor sleeps, if God sees all, it is a stunning thought that God loves me. He does, after all, see those thoughts and fantasies (and some actual behaviors as well) that I wish he didn't see, but despite all that, God loves even me. It staggers the mind. Even if I spit in God's face, as I've done at times, he still loves me. God may not be happy at everything I am and do, but even seeing all, his love is undiminished. It motivates me to live according to God's ways—not to gain his love, for that is not in question, but to give him the joy that comes from gazing into the depths of an obedient heart.

೪ 122.1

I was glad when they said to me,
"Let us go to the house of the LORD."

I'm thinking that pilgrims to the Jerusalem temple were glad when setting out on their journeys, and even gladder when they arrived. I'm usually glad, too, when someone says, "Let's go to church." I'm glad because I love most of the people at church, and I love to sing the hymns, and I love God—or at least I think I love God, or I try to. And when I leave church, I nearly always feel better than when I arrived. I'm glad when I go to the house of the Lord.

Vast numbers of people feel otherwise. I read recently that most people born after 1960 are likely to be indifferent about the church, and those born after 1980 are likely to be downright hostile to it. Glad is not what they are when someone says, "Let us go to the house of the Lord." Why is that?

It's not, I feel certain, because younger adults lack a spiritual interest. I see lots of evidence of spiritual searching among people younger than me—in the self-help section of bookstores, the attendance at 12-step meetings, and the experimentation with drugs, therapies, and self-awareness seminars. Many young adults today long for what the institutional church has traditionally offered or claimed to offer—a grounding in a reality beyond this world. But they do not look for it in church. Why is that?

Could it be because church is boring? We do the same old things again and again, and while they are in many ways beautiful things, today's young adults, reared on "Sesame Street" and the "Electric Company," expect something with more energy. Could it also be because those of us within the church don't often manifest the all-embracing love of Christ in our lives? Could it be because young adults today find greater affirmation and acceptance elsewhere? Could Christ in fact be working more outside the walls that bear his name than within them?

❧ 122.6

Pray for the peace of Jerusalem:
"May they prosper who love you."

Where is Jerusalem, the city of *shalom*, of peace, of well-being? Where is the city of God?

Jerusalem is, of course, an actual city in the Judean hills, 20 miles west of the Jordan River. At its center is Mount Zion, sacred to Jews as the site of the temples of Solomon, Zerubbabel, and Herod, and to Muslims as the spot from which the prophet Muhammed departed for his night journey into heaven and the site of a Muslim architectural masterpiece. Jerusalem is also where the trial, crucifixion, and resurrection of Jesus occurred. The city is therefore a holy city for three faiths. But it is not today a peaceful city. Jerusalem is a disputed place, like a frayed rope in a tug-of-war game. Not only its current inhabitants, but people from around the world bicker over its status and fate. This psalm was originally sung by pilgrims on their way to Mount Zion. We can sing it even now for the inhabitants of that holy city, and for its pilgrims.

For Christians, the church is also the city of *shalom*, the city of God. A popular visual image of the church is the ark, providing a safe haven for God's creatures. But like the actual city of Jerusalem, today the church is not always a safe and peaceful place. Interest groups and partisan debaters defame one another at church councils in the name of the Prince of Peace, bloodying the floors of church halls. We can sing and pray this psalm for our church.

Finally, each Christian soul is the city of *shalom*, the city of God. Like the actual city and the church, the souls of Christians are to be at peace with God and the world. Yet we experience turmoil within. Anger, confusion, bitterness, boredom, fear—any of these may give rise to strife in the soul. Peace comes through surrender of the will to God, even when we cannot see where the next step will take us. This psalm can be the prayer of every spiritual pilgrim on the windy, rocky road to the Kingdom.

℘ 123.1

To you I lift up my eyes,
  to you enthroned in the heavens.

Me, too. I lift up my eyes to God, quite often, in fact. I seem perpetually to be thinking of God—talking to God, listening for God, wondering about God. The awareness of eternity is always with me, even in my times of doubt. My problem is not that I may forget to lift up my eyes to the one enthroned in the heavens, but that I may be so taken with things heavenly that I neglect things earthly. To be called "starry-eyed," is not a compliment, but suggests an excessive other-worldliness that fails to take account of earthly reality. That could be me.

God invites us to love him, but that love is expressed in this world. God became a human being in order to meet us where we are. I suppose he could have transformed us into heavenly beings to meet him where he was, but that was not what God did. If we would meet God, we must meet him here. Jesus' parable of the Great Judgment (Mt. 25:31-46) could hardly be more clear. If we are to serve Jesus, we do it by serving the needs of his brothers and sisters here on earth, not through esoteric flights into heavenly realms. This requires us to get our hands dirty. As the hymn says, "How shall we love thee, holy hidden Being, if we love not the world which thou hast made? Bind us in thine own love for better seeing thy Word made flesh, and in a manger laid."

At the same time, we must not become so taken with things of this world, even laudable things, that we forget about God. I suppose a kind of dual vision is needed, eyes lifted up to heaven while at the same time focused on the details of faithful living in this world. Only when we raise up the poor and downcast, when we pray and strive for justice and peace, will God's kingdom come on earth, as it is in heaven.

ଓ 124.1a

If the Lord had not been on our side...

I've never known just what the word depression means when used of a person, but years ago, I think I sank into one. I couldn't sleep and I was barely going through the motions at work. I felt abused, angry, frightened, and desperately alone. I withdrew from those who loved me. Ominous clouds appeared on my mental horizon in every direction. Darkness surrounded me. And worst of all, I saw no chance of escape.

I was wrong about the last part. There was the possibility of escape—eventually *dawn happened*. I say it that way because for a time, I wasn't sure what or who had brought about the dawn. I knew things were better because I felt I'd been sprung free from a snare, but what made things better, who had sprung me from the snare, I didn't know. Dawn just happened—but where had the dawn come from? I couldn't say at the time what now seems obvious: *God brought the dawn.*

This psalmist is celebrating not a personal escape, but an escape of his entire nation. While he was probably thinking of the deliverance of the children of Israel from Pharaoh, it could have been a threatened invasion, epidemic, economic or political crisis, or national scandal. But then came the unforeseen miracle, the Red Sea, the covenant of Sinai, the cloud by day and the fire by night, the manna in the wilderness—*dawn happened.* During much of that time (if we're talking about the children of Israel and Pharaoh), the people couldn't or wouldn't see the Lord and turned from him. Only now, some years later, can the psalmist look back at his people's deliverance and say, "If the Lord had not been on our side, then... then...then..."

But the Lord was on their side. The Lord was on my side, too, though I couldn't see him during the time of my darkness, perhaps because I had turned my back on him. And the Lord is on your side, whether you see him or not. Wait for him.

○R 125.4

Show your goodness, O LORD, to those who
are good
and to those who are true of heart.

Some questions:

Who is good? As I see it, we're all a mixture of good and bad, and sometimes it's hard to tell what attitudes, motives, and behaviors distinguish goodness. Does some of it depend on the situation? The good people would be those who best reflect the nature of God in their lives, and we do know something about the nature of God, or at least we can know if we truly want to know. Even so, however, my knowledge of other people is limited, and unless we're considering Adolf Hitler and Mother Teresa, I have trouble sorting out who's good and who's bad.

What does God's goodness look like? Gobs of gourmet food, rooms full of gold, endless pleasures? The Book of Revelation has a bit of that in its more crass passages. But surely the greatest blessing God can bestow on anyone is the assurance of his power and love, something the good already know about. So God's goodness shown to the good would be nothing more than a further granting of a gift already abundantly given.

Why are we asking God to show his goodness to those who are good? Surely it's not as a reward. Didn't that notion go out a long time ago? God sent his Son to forgive us our sins and heal us so that we could stop worrying about making a perfect score on the goodness test. Could we be asking God to show his goodness to those who are good in order that others, seeing in them the joy of knowing and serving God, may be drawn to God?

Finally, what about the bad? Don't we want God to show his goodness to them as well? When we pray for world peace and justice, are we not asking God to show his goodness to the bad, to transform those who make war and protect the interests of the powerful, so as to change them and bring them to joy and truth?

ೞ 126.6

Those who sowed with tears
will reap with songs of joy.

Why would one weep while planting seed? Planting seed is usually done hopefully, in anticipation of a harvest. Perhaps the seed was sown as a last gasp effort when all seemed lost. There is no guarantee when sowing seed; not all seed brings in a harvest. The possibility of drought and crop failure is very real, or persons wishing to destroy us can frustrate our efforts and destroy our crops. Not everyone who sows will reap with songs of joy.

The psalmist recalls the time of the Exile, when all seemed lost, and if the people planted anything, it was in foreign soil where they wept whether or not the seed brought in a harvest. But then the Lord restored the fortunes of his people, and their mouths were filled with laughter. Now, though, hard times have returned. The psalmist ponders life's uncertainties, its ups and downs. It is amidst these fluctuations in fortune that he writes his song.

Unlike some others, he utters no cry of abandonment, but prays in simple trust that the Lord will once again restore the fortunes of his people.

Thinking back to the past informs his prayer. When circumstances are grim or frightening, the memory of an earlier, happier time can give hope, reassuring us that our present distress is not the all-encompassing reality it seems to be. The word of the Lord can come to us through the gift of memory. This includes both our personal memories, and the corporate memories of the church, told in its stories of God's goodness and grace long ago.

The psalmist also trusts the good he sees in the past. This is a decision. Two people looking at the same facts often reach opposite conclusions. One sees a glass half full while the other sees a glass half empty. What you see is a choice. Faith, in the sense of trust, is a choice. We can choose whether the darkness or the light will define us. Healthy prayer includes trust, or at least the hope, that despite the present darkness, light will return.

ൡ 127.1

Unless the LORD builds the house,
their labor is in vain who build it.

I had a good idea some years ago. The parish where I was rector had begun to grow and worship services were sometimes crowded. Four courses of action occurred to me: Found a new congregation, expand the building, add another worship service, or do nothing. For various reasons, I felt adding a worship service was the best choice. Moreover, children had been excluded from the main worship service (their Sunday School ran concurrently with worship) and I saw an additional service as an opportunity to welcome children to worship. It would also open a window to introduce alternative kinds of music and liturgy. Accordingly, I introduced an additional service designed to meet these needs. After a few months, however, attendance at the new service was so small that we dropped it.

Why had the new service failed? Thinking back, I realized I hadn't built support for the service among the people of the parish. In fact, I hadn't even asked them for an opinion. But there was also a deeper reason. Since the new worship service had been my idea, I had taken ownership of it. I was determined it would succeed. I was committed to it not so much because it was a *good* idea (although I still think it was), but because it was *my* idea. I hadn't differentiated my self from my idea—if the new service succeeded, I would succeed; if it failed, I would fail. Where was God in all this? The problem was that, for me at least, God wasn't in it at all. It was my idea, my project, my show.

How do we make certain that our labor is the labor of the Lord, that the Lord is building the house we're working to construct? One way is to honor the rest of God's people by consulting them and taking them seriously. A second way is to recognize that the important thing is not that this or that project succeed, but that we surrender our hearts and wills to God.

❧ 128.6a

May you live to see your children's children.

My wife and I have three grown sons, but no grandchildren as of this writing. But we would like grandchildren. Why are grandchildren so important to people? Part of it, certainly, is the pleasure grandchildren give. Our children gave us pleasure, too, but it was accompanied by great responsibility. Grandparents usually have the pleasure without as much responsibility.

Another part of it, I suspect, is the notion that grandchildren will carry on our name, our legacy, our identity. But in the modern world, children and grandchildren usually establish their own identities, often far from the communities in which they were reared and where their aging parents reside. Multi-generational ties are not what they once were. The idea that future generations will perpetuate our identity is illusory today, and perhaps it always was.

Some single persons and childless couples discover something parents and grandparents may overlook, that producing progeny isn't the most important thing. The human race requires progeny if it is to survive, but there is no reason a specific person needs to become a parent or grandparent. Some people become so focused on children and grandchildren that they lose their own sense of personal identity. The failure to differentiate ourselves from our children can become a problem both for them and for us. There are many ways to live productive lives, to love and serve God, to become a force for good in the lives of others, to offer a contribution that makes the world a better place—and many of them do not include having children or grandchildren of one's own.

It is very well to wish for grandchildren, as this psalmist does. It is not good, however, to hang too much on them. Let us learn to love and serve God in the circumstances where we find ourselves, among those near us, regardless of whose children and grandchildren they are. Those who discover how to do this in a way that is right for them are the truly blessed.

৩ 129.2

Greatly have they oppressed me since my youth,
but they have not prevailed against me.

I once knew a woman who spent thirty years in and out of psychotherapy, treatment centers, and relationships that didn't work. She attempted suicide more than once and ended up divorced from her husband, estranged from her children, and (except for paid therapists) friendless. As she saw it, she had been victimized all her life. Innocent herself, others had misunderstood, mistreated, and taken advantage of her. Her unhappiness was always the fault of someone else—her husband, her husband's family, her parents, her brother, her friends who failed to support her in her struggles. In fact, however, the woman had it backwards—it was she herself who had misunderstood, mistreated, and manipulated. The woman's real problem lay within her. It was a pervasive and persistent anger (she remembered minor slights for decades) that caused her to alienate family and friends.

I was not familiar with everything in the woman's life, either growing up or in her later marriage. There may have been abuse of some kind, particularly in her family of origin. Undoubtedly, she sometimes received less than her due. She could probably have latched onto this verse as a kind of mantra—but if reciting that mantra fed her sense of victimhood, it would not have helped, for she needed to put her oppressed youth behind her and move on. This can be hard to do for those burdened by terrible things, remembered or imagined, but somehow, we need to grow beyond our terrible things. The woman was unable or unwilling to do that, and as a result, her oppressions, real or imaginary, dominated her life. Because she clung to them, they determined who she was. Only when we move our oppressive memories and imaginings to the sidelines and step beyond them can healing take place. Then and only then can we truly say, "they have not prevailed against me."

☙ 130.1

Out of the depths have I called to you, O LORD;
LORD, hear my voice;
> *let your ears consider well the voice of my*
> *supplication.*

Verbal transcripts often don't tell you what you want to know. The meaning of spoken words can lie more in the facial expressions, body language, and tone of voice than in the words themselves.

Perhaps the words in this verse were muttered in a whisper: "I can hardly open my mouth, much less call for help. All my energy has been drained away. Everything looks dark to me. I hurt all over. All I can to is groan and moan. But you, Lord, know the meaning of groans and moans. You will hear me and understand what I cannot say. Lord, hear my voice and let your ears consider well the voice of my complaint."

Perhaps these words were roared in fear or anger: "I am about to go under, Lord! I'm struggling and fighting and screaming, but no one helps me! Listen to me, Lord! Pay attention to me!"

Perhaps they were uttered out of guilt: "I brought this on myself, Lord, and I deserve nothing good from your hand. I did what I should not have done, and have brought myself to this sorry place. But you are a merciful God, or so they say—and I want to believe it. So listen to me, Lord. Let the words of my supplication come to you. Then heal me and forgive me."

Perhaps they were spoken in confusion: "Why is all this happening? What's going on? I don't understand this. What do these things mean? How could such things happen to me? I'm not even sure what actually is happening. I don't know where I am any more or where I'm going. And I feel as if I am sinking, Lord, about to be swallowed up. Are you there, Lord? Where are you? Please don't let me die here, Lord. Hear me, come to me, save me!"

How have you spoken such words? And how did the Lord respond to you?

‹⋙ 130.3

For there is forgiveness with you;
therefore you shall be feared.

Most people are relieved to learn that God forgives sin. If they fear God, it is a fear of what God might do if he refuses to forgive sin. Why would this psalmist suggest that we fear God *because* there is forgiveness with God?

Because we know that God knows? To be forgiven is not the same thing as to get away with something. We can't get away with anything because God, knowing our thoughts even before we think them, sees not only what we do but our motives in doing it. All our pretenses are shattered. We stand naked before God. It may be good news, but forgiveness is also scary.

Because God might try to change us? Change is part of forgiveness. God doesn't merely say, "That's okay and I'll just pretend you never had those rotten thoughts." Rather, God says, "That's not okay, and I'm going to give you the opportunity to embrace different thoughts. Let me transform your mind. Let me lead you from death to resurrection. What's your answer?" This makes us afraid because, rotten though our old thoughts may have been, they are familiar and dear to us. At best, we are torn over how to respond to God. We'd like it both ways—retain our old selves and at the same time enjoy the blessings God offers. But we can't have it both ways, and that's scary.

Because God might forgive others just as he forgives us? It's all very happy that God forgives us and welcomes us into fellowship with him, but is God also going to forgive our dishonest competitor, our arrogant colleague, our irascible boss, the boring woman down the street, the man at the gym who taunts us? If we accept God's forgiveness and take our seat at God's table, will we have to sit next to those people? That prospect frightens us because we're not sure we can do it. Maybe we don't want forgiveness after all. Just leave things as they were.

❧ 130.4

I wait for the LORD; my soul waits for him;
in his word is my hope.

The opening verse of this psalm expresses a sense of darkness that could lead to despair, but a note of hope quickly emerges and grows stronger with each succeeding verse. The hope is not based on some new bit of news that suggests circumstances are improving, but on waiting—and not for news, but for the Lord. Waiting for the Lord can only occur when we have relinquished our control and our attempts to control.

My grandmother died at the age of 101. Earlier in her life, she had been a driving, opinionated, controlling woman, not inclined to wait for anything. My grandmother had been one who decided what should happen, then made sure it did. But during the last quarter of her life, while she was still alert, she began to soften. Then, during her final years, her mind faded until finally she knew no one and was conscious only of the present moment. Although I know she would not have chosen to forget the names and faces of those who loved her, I witnessed at the end of her life a further growth in the contentedness and happiness that had begun when her mind was still clear. The reason, I think, was that she had at last become willing to be and let be. Witnessing the change in her mental capacities frightened me in some ways, but in other ways it inspired me. My grandmother had learned to be still. She had learned to wait for the Lord.

Passivity is not always a good thing—some times call for action, and losing one's mind is, surely, not something to pray for. But in enigmatic and often frightening ways, God leads us where we need to go. Despite her diminished mental capacities, I cannot regard my grandmother's final years as "the depths" to which this psalmist refers in his opening verse. Mysterious and uncanny though they were, they were also years of grace, as if the tale of her life had finally arrived at the place intended for it.

♋ 131.2

I do not occupy myself with great matters,
or with things that are too hard for me.

And what would these "great matters" be?

Figuring out the mysteries of the universe, for one thing. I tried that. I read lots of books and thought deep thoughts, but the mysteries of the universe grew more mysterious, not less. I've concluded that not understanding things is part of who I am. It isn't going to change, so I accept it. If asked to state the meaning of life, I would once have given an answer, but now I'd more likely say, "That's a good question."

Politics and social issues, for another. Like most

people, I have opinions about those things. As I've grown older, I've become more politically and socially liberal, but I've also learned that nobody has all the solutions to such problems, least of all me. I once argued heatedly about politics and social issues, but when faced with an opinion with which I disagree, I'm now more likely to say, "That's an interesting viewpoint. Why do you feel that way?"

Telling other people what to do and think, for another. I'm less likely than I once was to try to run other people's lives for them, because I don't know what other people should do—and now I know that I don't know. Besides, people don't really want me to tell them what to do, even when they ask my advice. The most I'm likely to say now is, "Have you considered such-and-such as a possible course of action?"

If I don't occupy myself with great matters, then with what do I occupy myself? Small matters. Like being content with who I am. Like giving thanks for undeserved blessings. Like taking time to tell those around me how much they mean to me. Like doing the things God enables me to do to glorify and enjoy him and to make his world a more humane and gracious place.

But I still my soul and make it quiet,
like a child upon its mother's breast;
my soul is quieted within me.

The passionate energy of youth is a good thing. Without it, many an injustice would go uncorrected and many a noble endeavor unattempted. During my own youth, I set out to reform the world and bring the world to the truth.

It didn't work out that way. For one thing, as I grew older, I became less certain what the truth was, and for another, even when I thought I knew the truth, I lacked the energy, the courage, or the know-how to bring the world to it. While I hope I have been able now and then to influence someone for good, the world is much as it was before I launched my campaign to save it from error, and I recognize that I shall not change it. It's a complex mess of injustices and vanities, with a number of flashes of goodness mixed in. I suppose it always was this way and always will be. It was never my job to save the world, anyway. I now realize the world belongs to God. When and if the world needs changing, it is God who will change it, perhaps through me, perhaps in spite of me.

In place of the energy of youth has come the contentment of age. This, too, is a good thing. It gives permission for people to grow and change at their own pace, in their own way, which is more likely to be God's pace and God's way than if I forced my noble ideas upon them. If the danger of youth is puffed up and unrealistic ambition, the danger of old age is complacency. I hope I shall never grow complacent, but I have learned to be still, to rest on my mother's breast and allow my soul to be quiet within me. I continue to work and pray for a better world, but I no longer focus on results. I am content simply to be who I am and to let God be who God is.

ଔ 132.14-15

For the LORD has chosen Zion;
he has desired her for his habitation:
"This shall be my resting-place for ever;
here will I dwell, for I delight in her."

Zion is the name of the hill in Jerusalem to which King David took the ark of the covenant and on which three successive temples were erected. Many passages in the Psalms and elsewhere speak of Zion as the Lord's chosen dwelling, dear to him, and destined to triumph forever over her enemies. Such words probably expressed their authors' belief that the chosen people would for endless generations gather around Mount Zion in peace, security, and prosperity. Yet today, there is hardly a more disputed and volatile spot in the world. Must we then dismiss ancient hymns such as this one as naive, xenophobic illusions?

There may be elements of naive xenophobia in such writings, but they also contain insights into the heart of God, of which their authors were perhaps unaware. If Zion is the Lord's "resting-place for ever," then God is resting there even today, despite the seething conflicts between Jews, Christians, and Muslims, all of whom claim to follow him. God "rests" in the midst of the conflicts, and if God "delights" in Zion, there must be something even in that cauldron of contention which gladdens his heart. As Christians, we look to Jesus for the fullest disclosure of who God is, and we find in Jesus not a God reigning in regal splendor (though some psalmists and later Christians have envisioned God that way), but a God who stoops to his people, lives with and among them, shares their toil and heartache, bleeds with every one. However cacophonous may be the voices raised around Mount Zion today, God not only hears them all, but delights in each one as the voice of his own beloved child. The Lord is still present on Mount Zion. Perhaps he is more present there today than ever before.

❧ 133.1

Oh, how good and pleasant it is,
  when brethren live together in unity!

This paean to harmonious relationships compares unity to fine oil on the head (signifying kingship—and perhaps an ancient version of after-shave or perfume?) and to dew on the heights of a mountain. Heady images—but how exactly does one create unity?

Not by convincing everyone to agree. I've tried lots of ways to get people to agree with one another (and with my point of view)—arguing, cajoling, humor, bringing in high-powered experts. Nothing works. A few people might budge, but getting everyone to agree isn't going to happen, whether you're talking about something as complex as economic policy or as simple as what to serve for dinner. People are different, always have been, always will be.

Not by subjugation. For much of its history, the church executed people who didn't accept its official theology. Military despots have done the same. Individuals have also abused and dominated one another. That can produce a quiet scene, but one laden with smouldering resentments and unresolved tensions. Whatever that is, it isn't unity.

Not by pretending that differences don't matter. When two parties both feel entitled to the same thing, whether a parcel of land or a privilege, it doesn't do to say to them, "It's not all that important." They wouldn't be squabbling about it if it weren't important to them.

Harmony in human relationships can only occur when each person feels valued. We are willing to forego what we want when we feel we have been heard and taken seriously. In the personal sphere, this means honoring children, the aged, employees, servants, and others often overlooked. In the wider world, it means honoring every social, ethnic, national, and economic group and showing favoritism to none. To my knowledge, this has never happened in the history of the world. This psalm may be a pipe dream, but dreams can't come true until we dream them.

෬ 134.1

Behold now, bless the LORD, all you servants
of the LORD,
you that stand by night in the house
of the LORD.

This verse brings to my mind a memory from long ago. I have often attended evening worship services, some of them glorious, and stood in the chancel or the pew. Some of those times I remember with delight, but the memory this verse evokes is one of standing in a darkened church in the middle of the night, all alone.

I was confused, anxious, restless. Having lain awake for hours in the middle of the night, I finally got out of bed, dressed, and drove to the church. I entered and stood in the back of the church, entirely alone. With the darkness hiding most of the visual symbols that filled the church, and with no sounds of organ or singing or ruffling of pages, I noticed other and more subtle stimuli which I would normally have overlooked. A streetlight gleaming through a stained glass window. The sound of an auto horn in the lane. The faint smell of musty carpet. Creaking floorboards beneath my feet. The moon shining through an upper window and reflecting off a white hymnboard. My own breathing. Alone but for God, I prayed, sang hymns I had committed to memory, wept, shrugged my shoulders. I thought of the people who sat in those pews on Sundays—good people, mostly, some searching for they knew not what, some who had found it, and a few who seemed never to have lost it. I heard their singing and their laughter. I felt their arms around me. I had the sense that having left my house and driven to the church, I had come home. Then I chuckled. Finally, I laughed out loud. My problems were not solved during those moments standing alone in the church that night, but I realized in the darkness and the quiet that tomorrow, this place would still be there, the people would still be there, I would still be there, and God would still be there. Realizing that much, I needed nothing more. I sang another hymn, said a prayer of thanks, returned home, and dropped off to sleep.

℞ 134.2a

Lift up your hands in the holy place and bless the LORD.

I took part in a renewal weekend a few years ago that included a number of deaf people. The deaf signed the words to the songs as the rest of us sang them, and we soon learned to sign the songs ourselves. "Alleluia" and "hosanna" were two common words in the choruses of these songs, and a single sign served for both words—holding the hands above the head and moving them in a circular motion. We were constantly raising our hands and waving them in the air.

Midway through the weekend, I realized that a few days earlier, I would have been loath to raise my hands in the air while singing "Alleluia." Yet here I was doing exactly that, feeling not the least self-conscious, and having a very good time. What had changed me? Was the Holy Spirit rattling my cage? Possibly so. It wasn't that I was being nudged to alter my preference for traditional hymnody. Still less was I being told that from now on I was to raise my hands in the air whenever I praised the Lord. Rather, I was being given a glimpse into the hearts of my fellow Christians who regularly praise God in this way.

I had been uncomfortable raising my hands in worship because I had assumed raising one's hands in the air was a coded gesture indicating something more than a desire to praise God. It felt to me like a badge that identified members of a fraternity—from which I was excluded unless I bought into a set of theological positions I couldn't accept. I felt pressured to fit into a mold that made me uncomfortable. As I usually do when I feel like that, I resisted.

But could I have misconstrued the motives of hand-raising Christians? Could they have been merely praising God with hands as well as voices, as I had done with my new deaf friends? And was there any reason why I could not raise my hands with those for whom that gesture was a natural and spontaneous act of praise the next time I worshiped with them? Could the problem have been not with others and their expectations of me, but with me and my prejudices?

℀ 135.6a

The LORD does whatever pleases him, in heaven and on earth.

Among the things mentioned in this psalm which the Lord did, presumably because they pleased him, are sending rain to the earth, killing children, overthrowing nations, killing kings, and taking land from one people and giving it to another. The rain was presumably a blessing to all, but what about those other divine acts? Seen within the context of the Lord's choosing of Israel to be his people, there is a certain rationale to the Lord's behavior, but how does this Lord come across to the mother of a slain Egyptian boy or to a Canaanite herdsman driven from his land by Israelite invaders? Throughout the Bible, in fact, God acts in ways that could seem cruel and arbitrary. Did God really tell Abraham to kill Isaac? If God hardened Pharaoh's heart, why was Pharaoh punished for having a hard heart? What kind of God would torture Job just to prove a point to one of his heavenly attendants? And doesn't God's demanding the death of his Son to satisfy divine justice suggest a warped sense of justice? In short, is this the sort of God we want to worship?

Some have said no. Skeptics have portrayed the God of the Bible as fickle, even diabolical, and they easily amass biblical texts to support their view. But of course, scripture more often portrays God as merciful and just. So what is God up to, exactly? The honest answer is that we don't know. There are hints or pointers that suggest God is working out his purposes through events in the world, that everything that happens contributes in some way to God's purposes, and that God's purposes are good. But how specific events fit into those purposes, we cannot know. We—and the biblical authors—sometimes fail to recognize God's ways. We see only glimpses of what God is up to and we make mistakes in interpreting what we see. Yet we trust that God is good and that while we may not know what God is doing, God knows what God is doing. Such trust is a choice and a risk, but sometimes that is as far as we can go.

❧ 135.18

Those who make them are like them,
and so are all who put their trust in them.

This is the concluding verse of a passage that satirically mocks idolatrous worship. It may have been a well known bit of verse in ancient times, for the same words, somewhat expanded, appear in Psalm 115. The import of the passage cannot be missed: Idols are the works of human hands. Human artisans have given them mouths, eyes, and ears, but they cannot speak, see, or hear since they are lifeless objects. They are, in short, molded rocks, nothing more. This final verse makes the further point that anyone who devotes his life to a molded rock isn't much smarter than a molded rock himself—we become what we worship.

It is an easy thing to agree with the psalmist that asking favors and blessings from a statue is a dumb thing to do. It would not occur to modern people to pray to a statue. But idolatry is more subtle than that. The question is not to what or whom we address our prayers, but to what or whom we devote our lives. Look at your check stubs or your date book for an objective measurement of where your heart is. Consider what you think about when your mind is free. Where do you spend your money, your time, and your thoughts? For what end do you do what you do? Is the thing you love most something made and shaped by human hands? Is your highest value something rooted merely in this passing world, something that will be gone and forgotten shortly after, or even before, you are gone and forgotten? Though held in esteem by the world, is your chief love a pretentious bauble? We become what we worship, so those who worship pretentious baubles become pretentious baubles.

Idolaters don't have to remain idolaters. Conversion is always a possibility. If your life is empty and drab, consider conversion. Conversion may be spontaneous or gradual, but it is always an act of God. We don't change ourselves—God changes us. But conversion requires willingness on our part to be changed. Are you willing? Is this the time? What holds you back?

ॐ 136

...for his mercy endures for ever.

This psalm is a litany designed to be sung in worship, with the litanist singing the first half of each verse and the congregation joining in the repeated refrain. For years I thought this a dull psalm because the same short sentence ended every verse. I wanted to say, "Okay, I've got it—now let's move on to something else!" But I have come to see the value of repeating the psalm's key thought again and again. The very act of repetition seems to make it real—we don't move on to something else because God doesn't move on to something else.

The word translated mercy (sometimes as grace or love) is *hesed*, pronounced with a guttural *h*. It combines two ideas, so I prefer a translation which uses two words, rendering it "steadfast love." *Hesed* is seen in the Lord's election of the people of Israel on Mt. Sinai and his subsequent acts in delivering them from danger and settling them in the

Promised Land, a story told in the litanist's lines. The Lord does this because he loves his people. But equally important is the assurance that this love is steadfast, irrevocable, unchanging. Human love most nearly approaches this in marriage, where wife and husband promise "to have and to hold from this day forward, for better for worse, for richer for poorer, in sickness and in health, to love and to cherish, until we are parted by death." This is a love which, though often tested, is never defeated. It says, "I will be there for you until I die, whether I feel like it or not, whether it's fun or not, whether it's easy or not, whether I like you or not, whether you deserve it or not. You can count on me as long as there is breath in me. I will never leave you."

Apart from Christ on the cross, the Bible's most vivid illustration of *hesed* is in Hosea, where the prophet marries an incorrigible tramp but cannot stop loving her. This experience gives Hosea a piercing insight into the heart of God. The love of the people, like that of Hosea's wife, is like the dew that goes quickly away, but God's love "endures forever."

❧ 137.1,4

By the waters of Babylon we sat down and wept,
when we remembered you, O Zion.
How shall we sing the LORD's song
upon an alien soil?

This is one of the few psalms that can be dated with certainty. It comes from the sixth century before Christ, when the citizens of Judah had been carried into exile in Babylon. Their understanding of God and their relationship to God had been anchored to a sense of place, to their homeland, and especially to the Jerusalem temple, now destroyed. Their captors taunt them, asking that they sing what for them are sacred songs, merely for the amusement of those who know neither the songs nor the God worshiped in the songs. The crisis of faith which this occasioned is expressed in this psalm.

Modern Western Christians face a similar crisis of faith. Western culture was built around the church. A glance at the street plan of any medieval city will disclose a church or cathedral in the center, indicating the importance of the building and what took place there. No one questioned that God ruled the universe and that human social structures should express God's purposes. The church, as God's agent in the world, was the focal point of community life.

Although no geographical uprooting has occurred, the nature of the place where those churches and cathedrals still stand has radically changed. The buildings often seem like quaint anomalies today. The life of the modern city revolves around the skyscraper, the bank, or the shopping mall, not the church. Christian values are often mocked in the media and the public forum. To the committed Christian, soil once familiar has become alien; the memories of earlier times bring nostalgia, longing, and tears. Again the question arises: *How do we sing the Lord's song upon an alien soil?*

ℛ **137.9**

Happy shall he be who takes your little ones,
and dashes them against the rock!

Well, uh, yes, I suppose some people might find a certain happiness in dashing babies against rocks. "Working out my frustrations," they'd call it. The author of this psalm may have gotten this idea from reading Psalms 69 and 109, where vindictiveness oozes unrestrained. But at least in those psalms revenge isn't taken directly on innocent children (though the psalmists do want them orphaned). Those who thought it impossible to sink to a meaner vengefulness than that found in Psalms 69 and 109 may now want to reconsider.

Apart from the graphic image of babies being smashed against rocks, what makes this verse interesting is that we know what led to it. This psalmist's home and place of worship had been destroyed. Then he had been taken from their ruins to a foreign country and enslaved among people whose language he could not understand. Perhaps he had been separated from his family. He was bereft, as were all his friends, loved ones, and everyone he had known from home. The things that had given him and his community a sense of identity and purpose had all been stripped away. This is one of history's most shameful recurring themes, the ravaging of one people by another. It has happened in every age, but never with such chilling frequency as in the 20th century. And it is happening still, in the early days of the 21st century.

The result, seen in this psalm, is often (but not always) an irrational and frightening anger. While it may be possible on occasion to talk a victimized person out of such anger, it is better to eliminate the occasions which give rise to it. On a large scale, that would call for an even-handed and humane social policy, and on a small scale, for treating everyone with whom we come into contact with fairness, generosity, and grace.

ɷ 138.9

The LORD will make good his purpose for me;
O LORD, your love endures for ever;
do not abandon the works of your hands.

What is God's purpose for me? I once thought it had to do with what I accomplished in my life, with achievements for the benefit of the world and the good of God's people. Now, however, as most of my achievements are either behind me or will never come to pass, I see God's purpose differently. I believe God's purpose for people is that we may know, love, and enjoy him as he knows, loves, and enjoys us. It is a relationship thing, not an achievement thing. When we turn our backs on God, we thwart that purpose.

Is this thwarting of God's purpose permanent or temporary? We cannot know for certain, and one may cite scripture passages to support either position. But I like this verse's suggestion that God's purpose for us will ultimately prevail. Even if we persist in denying God until we die, God will not deny us. It is not in God to deny us. God's love endures forever, whether we live or die and whether we heed or ignore God. Nothing is stronger than the love of God;

nothing outlasts the love of God. God will not be denied forever.

So what happens to those who go to their graves without accepting God's love? Again, we do not know, and we must resist the temptation to make pronouncements about what is known only to God. But we entrust the dead, as we entrust the living, to a God whose love endures forever. I believe God will make good his purpose for us, if not in this life, then in the next. If there is a hell, I believe it is not eternal, but a kind of training room, a place where further growth and refining of our souls occurs until, at the last, we take our place in the arms of God.

ଔ 139.6

Where can I go then from your Spirit?
where can I flee from your presence?

This psalm is often read as a message of reassurance to those who feel cut off from God. It's lofty vision of a God who sees everything and whose sway is infinite has strengthened many souls in dark times. But to someone seeking to hide from God, the psalm can be unsettling, even intimidating. It reminds me of the opening lines of the Episcopal eucharist: "Almighty God, to you all hearts are open, all desires known, and from you no secrets are hid." I do not find that a soothing thought.

Our response to this psalm depends on two things. The first is what we know of ourselves. Public confessions of sin spoken by the congregation as a whole are not specific to each sinner and therefore do not require us to peer intently into our own souls. But when we do look within, we are often shamed by what we find. Any honest self-examination will uncover thoughts, behaviors, and attitudes which we would prefer that God not know about. The fact that God does know and that we know God knows can frighten us.

The second thing that determines our response to this psalm is what we know of God. Many people know God only as Judge. Their sense of God is that of a stern and unforgiving taskmaster whose habit is to punish and to do it severely, even endlessly. God is indeed grieved and angered by our infidelity, and we must not pretend otherwise. God is our Judge—but not *merely* our Judge. Our Judge is also our Redeemer. Having seen all our tawdry secrets, God does what is necessary to set us right again. That is more than giving advice or commandments. It's more than pleading with us. It's more than fuming and snorting threats. God comes to us, in person, in the flesh, and at great cost, to blot out the stain, clean up the mess, and bring healing and joy to our souls.

ങ 139.13

I will thank you because I am marvelously made;
your works are wonderful, and I know
it well.

Many people look at a marvel of nature—majestic things like
a sunrise over the Grand Canyon, the Canadian Rockies, or
a coral reef, as well as small things like a spider web, a leaf, or
a pebble on the beach—and think how wonderful God is to
have dreamed up such things and created them. But when we
look at ourselves, no such thoughts occur to us.

All God's works are wonderful, and human beings are
among the most wonderful of all. We are marvelously made,
and it is good to thank God for making us what we are.
Among the features of human beings I find most marvelous
are these, all of which I believe we have in common with our
Creator:

Our creativity. God creates out of nothing, but from
what God creates, we create symphonies, houses, poems,
gardens, dreams, monuments, games, dishes of food, and the
bonds of love and friendship.

Our sense of humor. When we laugh at the absurdity
of our pretensions and see ourselves as comical, whimsical
creatures, we are very close to the heart of God.

Our capacity to give. Natural to God, giving is learned
behavior for us. Children may be charming (especially if they
are our own), but they are also selfish. As we grow older,
though, most of us become more like God, learning to share,
considering the needs of others, and putting the common
good ahead of individual good.

Our capacity to grow. We learn from our failures and mistakes and move beyond them. While the philosophers have said God is immutable, I doubt it. There is little in the Bible about a changeless God. I believe one of the things we share with God is that we grow in grace and relationship. In that sense, God is *not* the same yesterday, today, and forever, but always growing.

℘ 140.3

They have sharpened their tongues like a serpent;
adder's poison is under their lips.

What with Jesus having blessed the peacemakers and Paul having urged brotherly affection among Christians, you might think Christians would at least be polite to one another. But no, not anymore. I recall a time when regional and national church gatherings were like family reunions. You might not have been particularly fond of all the people there, but you enjoyed getting together and when differences arose, everyone maintained a civil disposition and spoke kindly to one another.

Then something happened. A series of controversies in the Episcopal Church (and similar ones in other Christian groups, I'm told) arose and killed the civil tongue. It started with something called the General Convention Special Program in the 1960s. Then came Prayer Book revision, followed by women's ordination. Now it's the place of homosexuals in church life. Church meetings are now often tense and rancorous. Name-calling is in vogue. On one side are the "revisionist, heretical, radical, relativist, secular, humanist biblical illiterates." On the other are the "ignorant, simplistic, fundamentalist, homophobic, rigid biblical literalists." Each of these terms is slung like a stone, intended to hit and wound those on the other side. It seems everyone wants to shout and no one wants to listen.

As I read church history, I realize this is not a new thing—Reformation era partisans insulted one another with withering sarcasm, and so did people during the 19th century Catholic revival in Anglicanism and the Modernist controversy a few decades later. Perhaps the civility I recall from my youth was a brief if blessed interlude in what is normally a bloody battle. I know one thing for sure—when the devil can get Christians to throw rocks at each other rather than pray and seek the will of the Lord, he dances a merry jig.

❧ 141.2a

Let my prayer be set forth in your sight as incense.

Some people think of prayer as asking for favors: Heal this hurt. Deliver me from this danger. Solve this problem. Guide me in this decision. There is nothing wrong with such prayer. It acknowledges our dependence on God and the Bible tells us to make our requests known to God. But when our prayer consists of *nothing but* asking for favors, I expect we run the risk of becoming tedious to God.

Prayer is meant to be a conversation between lovers. Lovers often ask things of one another and are pleased to give what is asked, but love is based on more than what each lover can get from the other. Those entering into a relationship only for what they can get out of it are not in love—they're in something else. Love is founded on devotion, trust, and respect. It is often expressed in giving with no possibility of getting anything in return. A lover may even give his or her beloved an anonymous gift just for the pleasure of seeing the beloved's happiness. If you're looking for a synonym for love, consider *commitment*. Love isn't a feeling, because feelings come and go. Commitment, though, remains. It encompasses all manner of emotions and moods.

Prayer expresses commitment. It includes thanks-giving, adoration, and confession as well as asking for favors. It includes joking and laughter. Prayer is often tender and gracious, but occasionally (as with conversation between human lovers) prayer can be angry, confused, or doubting. It can even include wailing and griping. Most important, it includes listening as well as speaking. Whatever else it is, prayer should always be honest.

Honest prayer has the sweet scent of incense. As incense rises through a church and banishes less agreeable odors, so honest prayer, devoid of pretense and guile, rises to heaven and rejoices the heart of God.

Set a watch before my mouth, O LORD,
and guard the door of my lips.

Apart from the occasional remark that is simply misunderstood, most of the trouble our mouths get us into derives from our insecurity. Unsure that our opinions will be valued, we belabor them. Unsure that our jokes will be appreciated, we follow our punch lines with blaring laughter of our own. Unsure what others think of us, we demean those not present. Unsure that others will recognize that we are insiders, we break confidences and reveal confidential information. And unsure of everything about ourselves, we sedate our feelings of insecurity by drinking to excess and allowing what guards we formerly placed upon our lips to lapse.

The secret to keeping a proper rein on our tongues is to look beyond ourselves. So long as we hanker for a reputation among our peers, our lips will betray us sooner or later. When we puff ourselves up with windy words and vain conversation, someone will invariably see through our pretenses to the shallowness within us. As we think we're growing larger in others' eyes, we actually grow smaller. It illustrates the paradox of the gospel: "He who finds his life will lose it, and he who loses his life for my sake will find it." (Mt. 10:39)

When we invite Christ to enter and possess our souls, things begin to take shape the way they're supposed to. By surrendering our wills to him, we make Christ the center for us and allow him to speak through us. We begin to look differently at other people, and their reputation begins to matter as much as our own reputation. It is likely that we will begin speaking less often and listening more. It is also likely that what we do say will be listened to as never before. "Take my lips and let them be consecrated, Lord, to thee."

☙ 142.3a

When my spirit languishes within me,
you know my path...

The best story I know of someone with a languishing spirit walking along a path was written over 300 years ago. It's called *The Pilgrim's Progress*, by John Bunyan. The reason I like the story so much is that it's my story. The fellow on the path is called Christian, but he rarely measures up to his name. He gets into a lot of trouble, and it is usually his own fault. Sometimes it's because he doesn't trust the right people. Sometimes it's because he doesn't pay attention. Sometimes it's because he can't figure out what's important and what's not important. In short, Christian is his own worst enemy.

But Christian knows where he wants to go and never quite loses sight of his destination. He enters into conversations with people who do him no good. He bumbles along and gets sidetracked. He gets scared. Sometimes he despairs—his spirit "languishes within" him, as the psalmist says—but he doesn't give up. By simple plodding, Christian manages to get through the Slough of Despond, By-path Meadow, Doubting Castle, the Valley of the Shadow of Death, Prating Row, and Vanity Fair. He is not swayed by Mr. Worldly Wiseman, Lady Feigning, Giant Despair, or Madam Bubble. Christian always keeps the Delectable Mountains, in Immanuel's Land, in view, and in the end, he arrives at the gate of the Celestial City where Shining Ones receive him and escort him to the place where he sees the Holy One "as he is."

The Holy One was, of course, with Christian all along the way and made certain that Christian met certain people at critical moments, people like Evangelist, Interpreter, and Hopeful. God knows where we are—"You know my path," as the psalmist says—because the Son of God has walked this way before us. We may at times fail to recognize him, but he is there, recognized or not, and he has sanctified every step of the way with his presence and holy tears. Even if we wanted to, we could not walk alone.

෬ 143.10

Teach me to do what pleases you,
for you are my God;
let your good Spirit lead me on level ground.

I am not the best student, Lord. My mind wanders in class. Sometimes I don't do my assignments. I fail to see the significance of things and how one thing relates to another. I often forget today what I learned yesterday and require remedial instruction. But you, Lord, are a good teacher. You know me. You know what I need to know, how I learn, and how to get my attention. You know me better than I know myself. And you are patient with me. You don't mind returning to the same lesson again and again. I can always trust you (though sometimes I don't). You are the best teacher there is, Lord.

So teach me, Lord, and lead me. If possible, lead me on level ground—I can do without steep hills and dangerous ravines. If I have a choice, I'll forego stress, disappointment, and confusion. Surely there's nothing wrong in praying for that, though I dare not expect it. It's what I'd like, so I'll go ahead and ask for it. But most of all, Lord, I want you to lead me in a way that moves and causes me to follow. If stress, disappointment, and confusion are required to drive me finally to follow, then so be it. When I don't want to go where you say, Lord, then do what you need to do to get my attention and to change my mind.

Make me to love what you love and to desire what you desire, so that I follow you freely and joyfully. I mean that, Lord, or I think I do—or at least, I mean it much of the time, or I want to mean it.

But what if I don't mean it? Then lead me against my will, Lord. Subdue me, overpower me. "Batter my heart, three-personed God," if battering I need. "Take me to you, imprison me, for I, except you enthrall me, never shall be free, nor ever chaste, except you ravish me."

ॐ 144.1a

Blessed be the LORD, my rock!

Actually, Lord, could we just skip the rock part? I know that lots of people, including several psalmists, like to think of you as a rock. It suggests reliability, steadfastness, or some such thing. That's okay in some situations—a rock is better than sand when you are building a house on it, Jesus said. But what if I fall and hit my head on the rock? I did that once when I was a youngster and split open my forehead. I don't want to do it again. Rocks don't have much give to them. If you don't mind, Lord, couldn't you be a cotton ball rather than a rock?

I have another problem with the rock thing, too, Lord. Even if you are my rock—strong, faithful, true—I've gotten in trouble when I've assumed that because I'm your guy (what with my being a Christian and all), I should also be a rock. I've sometimes said something like this to people: "You can't do (or say or believe) that, because that's not what God wants. God wants you to do (or say or believe) the same as I do. I know about God and what God wants, and it never changes. God's a rock, and so am I. You'll be a rock, too, if you're smart, just like God and me." I haven't made many friends talking that way, Lord, either for you or for myself.

The thought of you as a rock, Lord, also implies a certain sameness, a predictability, a static quality to our relationship. But surely you don't want me to be the same person today that I was yesterday, Lord. Verna Dozier tells of a hymn she sang as a child, "On Christ the solid rock I stand. All other ground is sinking sand." She says she liked the hymn as a child, but learned as an adult that the ground is always shifting and that she had to live with a certain tentativeness and uncertainty. That's what faith is all about. The lust for certitude is a form of faithlessness, she says. I've discovered the same thing, Lord. I think you're more like a river than a rock.

ᏟᎡ 145.2

Every day will I bless you
and praise your Name for ever and ever.

Some days it seems easy to bless the Lord. The sun is shining in my soul and gentle breezes blow. Prayer flows effortlessly. The right thing is clear and my desire to do it unclouded.

More often, though, something gets in the way. It may be my busyness—I find it easy to put off blessing the Lord when my calendar is crammed with appointments and deadlines. It may be my ignorance and confusion—when life's ambiguities and complexities make everything seem hazy, I don't know what blessing the Lord looks like. It may be my exhaustion—sometimes I seem to lack the energy even to open my Bible, to repeat the simplest prayer. It may be my boredom—sometimes I just don't care. And sometimes, I know, it is my disobedient soul following its own desires when it knows better.

How is it, then, that the psalmist can promise to bless the Lord *every day?* It is only possible, I think, with a prayer something like this: "Gracious, forgiving Lord: I offer myself to you, such as I am, and ask that you receive this offering, broken as it is. You have given this day to me; I now give it back to you. Sanctify my conscious thoughts, my unconscious motivations, my steps, my actions, my words. Work your will through me, or in spite of me, as it may be. I do not know who I am, what I do, where I go. I only know that you are with me and that I am yours. And knowing that, I know all things."

℘ 145.16-17

The eyes of all wait upon you, O Lord,
and you give them their food in due season.
You open wide your hand
and satisfy the needs of every living creature.

We think that our intelligence, ingenuity, cleverness, and hard work entitle us to material possessions, a satisfying job, recognition, and a good reputation. We rarely consider that intelligence, ingenuity, cleverness, and the ability to work are gifts from God. I once fancied that my having worked hard for an education should entitle me to something later in life. But I later came to see that my mind is a gift, as were the parents and teachers who encouraged me to study and learn to use my mind. Friends, family, and colleagues are gifts. That I have rewarding work is a gift. That I can speak and write is a gift. Every moment is a gift proceeding from the open hand of God. My very breath and heartbeat are gifts. We can make good use of the gifts God has given us, or we can squander them, but they are not ours. When we call something our own, it is a polite fiction, taken seriously only by recorders of deeds and officials at the Internal Revenue Service. This will become clear when we die, if not sooner. All is gift, neither earned nor deserved.

John Donne knew the truth that all comes from God. He wrote: "Nature reaches out her hand and gives us corn, and wine, and oil, and milk; but thou fillest her hand before, and thou openest her hand that she may rain down her showers upon us. Industry reaches out her hand to us and gives us fruits of our labour for ourselves and our posterity; but thy hand guides that hand when it sows and when it waters, and the increase is from thee. Friends reach out their hands and prefer us; but thy hand supports that hand that supports us."

❧ 146.1b

I will praise the LORD as long as I live;
I will sing praises to my God while I have
my being.

This psalmist is jubilant. For as long as breath is in him, he will sing praises to his God. Nor is he alone. Many religious folk like to sing God's praises. Singing is my favorite part of worship—there's too much talking and too little singing in church. I love the classic hymns and if there is a moment during worship when tears come to my eyes, it's usually during the singing of some hymn. I hope to sing praises to my God as long as I "have my being."

But I also know, as does the psalmist, that to sing praises to God is more than to croon a tune; it is an act of trust, an orientation of the will, reflected in the life we live. Our best praise is a life devoted to God's glory. It's one thing to sing out in church, but it's another to praise God with our lives. One can make a big show of singing divine praises but then worship and serve human powers—political, economic, social, psychological. Human powers are long on promises but short on delivery. They may offer a fleeting hope, but they lead ultimately down a dead end road. Like all created things, their power is derivative, dependent on One beyond themselves. This becomes clear in time, as they pass away, leaving little or nothing behind them. Security is found in trusting God, and nowhere else.

The psalmist knows that to live a life agreeable to God is a matter of justice to the oppressed, setting prisoners free, feeding the hungry. God has, in the words of Gustavo Gutierrez, a "preference for the poor." Earthly powers not only avail nothing, but are often on the wrong side, at cross purposes with God. Far from delivering the poor from privation, they protect the privileges of the prosperous, who then return the favor by using their influence to preserve the power of those who do their bidding.

Sing praises to God? By all means, but make sure you sing the right song.

❧ 147.3-4

He heals the brokenhearted
and binds up their wounds.
He counts the number of the stars
and calls them all by their names.

The last five psalms are all songs of praise, beginning and ending with the word "Hallelujah," meaning "Praise the Lord!" This psalm, and these two verses in particular, focus on the paradox of God's immanence and transcendence. On the one hand, God "heals the brokenhearted." Like a nurse or mother, God lifts us into his lap and enfolds us in his arms when our hearts are broken, and gently bandages our knee when we stumble on rough pavement. God restores body, soul, and mind. From no hurt, not even those caused by our own foolishness and willfulness, will God withhold his healing balm. Nor does God wait for us to call to him in our distress—so deep is God's love for us that God comes to us unbidden, seeks us when we are lost, even before we know we are lost, and suffers himself on our behalf. Tenderness and intimacy are the hallmarks of God's dealings with us.

On the other hand, God dwells in light inaccessible and realms inconceivable. His majesty and sovereignty surpass human imagination and there is "no limit to his wisdom" (vs. 5). From the largest intergalactic cluster to the tiniest subatomic particle, God dreams up everything that is, then fashions it according to his will and whimsy. Moreover, God knows the name of each of his creatures, names by the trillions of trillions. He calls each star by name (vs. 4), each grain of sand, every amoeba, every atom. Such is God's power and glory.

Why would this God, with an entire universe to amuse him, trouble himself to heal my broken heart and bind up my bleeding wound? I do not know why God does this. I only know that he does.

ℭ 148

Praise the LORD.

As the Psalter approaches the finish line, it shifts into high gear. The last few psalms were presumably chosen to cap the collection on what the anonymous editor(s) felt was the most fitting note—praise. Each of the last five poems in the collection is a hymn of praise. In this psalm, the natural order is bidden to join "all peoples" to praise the Lord. Angels, heavenly bodies, weather systems, living things of all kinds, peoples of various descriptions and stations—"let them praise the Name of the Lord."

Why praise? Not every psalm we have encountered has included praise (although a concluding sentence of praise was often added to an otherwise sultry text, almost as if to sanitize it). Gathered from various sources, the collection has ranged over the whole field of human emotions, from grief to joy, from confusion to comfort, from affliction to healing, from cursing to blessing. Nothing, however unsavory or unedifying, has been omitted. Can a few jubilant praise songs adequately conclude an anthology of poems so diverse as these?

The editor apparently thought so. This suggests something about what it means to "praise the Lord." Joy is surely a part of it, at least much of the time—a perpetually shriveled disposition hardly suggests praise. But no one is joyful all the time. Even persons of solid faith occasionally feel the ground giving way beneath them; even those who shine the brightest experience occasional moments of darkness. That dark feelings are included in the Psalter and not covered over suggests that this is natural, a part of every life, to be expected. It also suggests that it is possible to praise God even in the worst of times. Such praise may not be cheery, but apparently praise need not always be cheery. To praise God is to live faithfully, or as faithfully as we can, in the bad times as well as in the good times. It isn't a matter of happy moods—and perhaps the most profound praise of all is rendered at the moment all seems lost.

ೞ 149.4a

...the LORD takes pleasure in his people.

"Yes, you heard me right. I said 'pleasure.' Do you find that hard to believe?"

Well, Lord, it's just that I don't usually think of you as—well—having a *good time*. Pleasure seems so trifling for you, so beneath your dignity. I mean, you are the supreme Ruler of the universe, the Alpha and the Omega, the ultimate One—aren't you, Lord?

"Of course I am, and that means I can do whatever I please. I can have a good time if I want and no one can tell me I can't—don't you agree?"

I always agree with you, Lord, always. It's a policy of mine to agree with you. So if you want pleasure, go for it. I figure you're entitled to it. I know what gives me pleasure (we don't have to get into that here, do we?), but I'd be curious to know what gives *you* pleasure, Lord.

"You do. Not all the time, of course. There are moments when you don't give me any pleasure at all, when you make me mad or when you grieve me. But those moments are fewer than you might think. Most of the time I really like being with you. I enjoy hanging out with you. That's why I made you. I was lonely in my self-sufficient omnipotent infinitude. It was a burden to me and I had to figure out a way to get around it. So I came up with you. And I'm glad I did."

Really, Lord? You're *glad* you came up with me, after all I've done and all I've not done?

"I've had second thoughts now and then, but yes, I'm still glad I made you. You were a risk, to be sure, but one thing I've learned from you is that some risks are worth taking. Making you was a risk worth taking, and if I had it to do over again, I'd do it, only I wouldn't wait so long next time. To tell you the truth, I don't much enjoy your self-deprecating penance. I know you need to do that—it's good for your soul, so long as you don't do too much of it, so I let you do it, but I'm always glad when penance time is over and we can move on to something else. How about if you get your glove, and we'll play catch? Or shall we send out for a pizza?"

❧ 150.3-5

Praise him with the blast of the ram's-horn...with lyre and harp....with timbrel and dance...with strings and pipe....with resounding cymbals... with loud-clanging cymbals.

The last note of the Psalter is literally that, a note—or rather, a whole bunch of notes, blown and strummed and clanged on instruments of all sorts. I suppose this music was played in the temple or some other place of worship since that's where the Lord is typically praised.

Or is it? The prophets seem to suggest otherwise, with Micah shrugging off formal worship in favor of justice, kindness, and humility (Micah 6:8) and Amos even asserting that the Lord hates acts of worship when the worshipers neglect justice (Amos 5:21-24). Church-going is only a good thing when it reminds us of what God desires and strengthens our commitment to it, not when it serves as a substitute for it. Church attendance can feed hypocrisy if we don't listen to what we hear there and don't mean what we say there.

Whatever else the Psalter does, it makes hypocrisy in worship difficult. It has been called the hymnbook of the Jewish temple—and a strange hymnbook it is, including thoughts no serious Jew (or Christian) would want to commend. It is not surprising that modern Prayer Book editors have taken their scissors to the Psalter with a vengeance, snipping out long sections in what they assign for Sunday worship. If you want the whole message of the Psalms, you must read more than the passages favored by Prayer Book revisers, which tend towards sweetness and light at the expense of what they regard as unseemly or embarrassing.

And so we end with music—bold, blaring, brash music that is much like life itself. The Psalms, taken in their entirety, are much like life itself. So let the sounds come forth, discordant and distressing though some of them are. Praise the Lord, with whatever voice and words you find within you. Know that the Lord is good and that he loves you, even when you sing awful songs. Worship honestly; tell it like it is for you. If a change is called for, God will tend to it.